Roadmap to Financial Freedom

Skip Nichols

www.TotalPublishingAndMedia.com

ISBN 978-1-63302-022-1

Table of Contents

Foreward

Bill Parker, Executive Vice President, Phillips Petroleum

Working as a senior manager for a major energy company, I made decisions daily that impacted the financial success of the company. Having worked for the company many years, I was comfortable with my knowledge of the processes and tools available to insure the outcome of my decisions were an improved bottom line result. In return I received a good salary and the opportunity to invest in the company's retirement and stock savings plans.

While I was totally involved with the company's success, I treated my retirement and savings investments very passively thinking that smarter people would take care of me. Other than looking at a quarterly statement, I had little idea of the mechanics about investing. Then one day, a merger was announced, and retirement was now. After spending an hour with a human resources person, I discovered how poorly I was prepared for the financial decisions ahead of me. It was time to get educated and find someone to teach and guide me through these decisions.

I turned to a college friend, Skip Nichols, who had sold me some life insurance policies years ago. Skip's practice had grown from life insurance to financial investments plus he was a trusted friend of 30 years. He had developed a process called the Financial Lifestyle Plan that evolved into the Roadmap to Financial Freedom, and it became my Bible. I learned the phases of my financial life: wealth creation, wealth preservation and wealth transfer. I learned the tools of investment: equities, fixed income, ETFs, REITs and exotics such as covered calls and derivities. I learned the importance of advisors, not only financial, but tax, legal, estate and insurance. The Roadmap to Financial Freedom touches all the important aspects for someone facing financial decisions now or preparing for the future.

About the Author

James K. "Skip" Nichols, Chartered Financial Consultant

Skip's career, spanning over fifty years, has been built around helping people in financial services and informing them with sound money management principles. In 2008 he was nominated by ING Financial Partners as one of the Top Ten Financial Planners in America for business growth and community involvement. He has presented successful money management seminars at the University of Tulsa, and the Oklahoma University Dental School as well as for numerous corporations throughout America.

Chapter 1
Will my Money Last?

Many would say that Ted and Ruth Dunleavy are the picture perfect, all-American baby boomers. Ted was born smack in the middle of Korean War... August, 1951 to be exact. His dad, although fighting age, had to stay home from the big war because of a hernia. Detroit, Michigan was his birthplace and like so many other of the great American middle class it laid the foundation, the underpinnings, for the questions, optimism, and fears that he now faces some 64 years later.

Ted's childhood and early formative years are a mosaic of the American middle class. His Dad was born on a poor tobacco farm in Horse Cave, Kentucky. It is funny how we forget that the middle class way of life that we so much enjoy hasn't always been this way. Middle class in America is only about three generations old. The questions, optimism, and fears that he and Ruth face about retirement are relatively new questions.

Previous generations did not have these opportunities to plan their retirement... there wasn't a retirement as we think of it today. Only a few generations ago, when grandpa got too old, too feeble, too weak to work he was taken care of by the children. That was his retirement. He had no Social Security income, no 401(k), no pension, no second home in Florida to spend the winter.

So the thought, "if I retire will my money last?" has only been around for less than three generations. Biblical history goes back 5000 year; therefore, three generations isn't very far. Less than one percent of all the people who ever lived on our planet have ever had this question. You see how things are changing? Ted and Ruth have a great opportunity to spend the next 20 to 30 years in a comfortable, enjoyable, and worry free retirement. According to the 2000 actuarial study, their retirement years may be nearly as long as their working years. Do you see now why Ted is asking, "Will my money last as long as Ruth and I do?"

Ted has been dreaming of retirement for a long time. Dreaming of retirement seems to be a passion of this baby boom generation. As a financial planner, with 50 years of experience, it is interesting that the retirement planning of today is a rather new concept. I've read through the Bible several times and there is only one group, the temple priest of the Old Testament, who retired. What a cosmic shift in thinking! From the beginning of time until 100 years ago there wasn't retirement as we know it today in America. Now, people are developing retirement plans in their fifties. Here is where the story begins with Ted and Ruth. Let's sit in on the first meeting with them late last winter.

A client of our firm and a coworker of Ted referred Ted and Ruth to us. We met Ted and Ruth for the first time on a cold, windy day in January. Days in Oklahoma can change significantly during the winter. I remember on the day before they came in and it was 80°, yet the day we met the temperature was barely above 35°. The wintry, cloudy day hadn't cooled their excitement about potentially retiring on Ted's next anniversary.

Karen, our office manager, got them a cup of coffee and escorted them back to my office. After a few pleasantries I asked Ted and Ruth, "Help me to understand how we can help you". Ted answered in a steady yet questioning voice, "I've worked at Sunoco for the past 35 years. Ruth and I have a pension, a 401(k) plan, some savings and little debt. If at all possible I would like to retire at my next anniversary. But, I have this nagging fear, if I retire now will I run out of money? My friend Gary, who I work with at Sunoco, has told me you can help me answer this question."

It has now been a year since Ted and Ruth and I started their financial journey. As with all journeys there are unexpected curves, bumps and obstacles. During our journey we answered their initial question, "if I retire now will I run out of money"? With hundreds of other clients I've counseled through the years, I've found their question was only one of many which needed to be answered for them to develop a financial roadmap which would 'Get Their Financial House in Order'.

This book is about that "roadmap" and the process we should all take. You, too, can answer the question, how much in investments will

2

we need so we will never run out of money? As the financial planner, this is the primary question in people's minds when they come to see me. As we work together they learn there are many other areas to consider when facing retirement. Another question they should ask is how to get all my financial 'stuff' arranged properly? You probably have asked yourself, if every area of your financial life has been properly addressed and covered. What about the areas you don't know much about, such as wills, trust, asset allocation, proper insurance coverages and deductibles, beneficiary designations, income and estate taxes? Have you ever woke up at night wondering if this or that has been properly handled? The purpose of this book is to enable you to make sure "Your Financial House Is in Order." In the following pages we will cover these items:

Basics of Successful Retirement
Financial roadmap
Tax saving information..it's your money
Eight categories of insurance
Tools to protect and grow wealth
Asset allocation
Selecting a financial advisor
Wealth transfer process..Why is it so hard?
Your Family Meeting
Final destination
Personal financial data form

As we say in Oklahoma, saddle up, it may be bumpy but we are going to have a fun ride. Are you ready to begin your journey to "get your financial house in order"?

Source; Annuity 2000 Mortality Table; Society of Actuaries

Chapter 2
Basics of Successful Retirement

It is be in a year since our first meeting on that cold, windy day in January. I remember Ted's question as though he had ask it of me yesterday. "Skip", he said, "it's a mystery, I tell you it's a mystery." Frankly, he had caught me off guard with that statement. I replied, "Ted, what do you mean 'it's a mystery?'"

Ted leaned forward in his chair, planted both arms firmly on the roundtable we were sitting at and thoughtfully took a deep breath. "Mr. Nichols," Ted said in a sober voice, "I am an engineer by training and have spent my life doing calculations that need precise answers. Give me concrete items such as mass and volume and weight and I can come up with the answer to solve a problem. This retirement is a mystery though... there is no precise answer I can come up with. How long will Ruth and I live? What will inflation be? What rate of return will we receive on our investments? What will our health needs be? These are just a few of the unknowns. Do you see why I say it's a mystery?"

You have to love engineers. They think through problems and come up with solid concrete answers. In my 50 years in the financial services business I think Ted summed it up better than any lecture I had intended. He is right. Retirement planning, at first blush, is a mystery. Everything Ted said was exactly correct. People approaching retirement, like Ted, or already retired face increasingly complex challenges of planning for income to last throughout their lifetime. However, all is not lost. It is important to build a retirement plan and it can be done with a little time, a lot of awareness and some step-by-step assistance from your investment professional. By taking these steps you don't have to go into retirement totally confused or unprepared. We may not be as precise with our conclusion as Ted is after he does a complex geometric formula involving height and weight and volume; but we can come pretty close to planning a safe and secure retirement. Actually, we approach retirement planning much like Ted approaches an engineering problem. We go about it in a logical and systematic manner. The process we use involves these steps:

- gathering the data (i.e., assets, debts, sources and amount of income, etc.)
- goal setting (i.e., income needs during retirement, debt repayment, travel, etc.)
- assumptions (i.e., return on investments, inflation, etc.)
- projections (i.e. projecting the return on assets minus the withdrawals)

Building a retirement plan begins with gathering the data. In the appendix I have included the data form we use. You'll notice that it covers all areas of a person's financial life. After all, my job as a financial planner is to help people solve their problems. There's an old saying 'people don't know what they don't know.

It is shortsighted to address how much is needed for retirement and leave other financial areas un-addressed. Let me tell you a tragic example of 'not knowing what they don't know'. Recently we worked with an attorney who told me a heartbreaking story. The couple, in their mid-70s, had seemingly prepared well for retirement. They were living comfortably. Like many of us they were trying to cut down on their expenses and looking through their budget they decided they could eliminate a big insurance premium each year by cutting back on their automobile insurance. We all can just imagine the conversation around the kitchen table... "Honey, our auto insurance premium has gone up again this year. We don't drive the car very much anymore and besides it is 12 years old. It is only worth $3000 if it was totally destroyed. Why don't we reduce our coverage down to the minimum?" Not an unreasonable thought.

About three months later, the Mrs. was pulling out of the grocery store parking lot onto the main street of town. Unfortunately she didn't see the motorcycle that was approaching from her left. The motorcycle struck her car on the driver's side and catapulted him over the car 60 feet. The cyclist had severe head injuries and a broken back. Two years later, the Court awarded the cyclist and his family $800,000. The insurance company paid the $50,000 liability limit. Guess who was left to pay the other $750,000? Do you see why it is so important to address all financial issues and gather all data?

Gathering the data

I called gathering the data the 'grunt' work of retirement and financial planning. There is nothing easy or fun about it, but it is critical. My son Brian is an architect. He develops amazingly detailed plans. People will drive by his buildings and marvel at their beauty and functionality. When they start construction on the building what do they do first? They lay the foundation. They dig in the ground and it is dirty and hard work. Gathering the data for your financial and retirement plan is like that. You have to hunt for information and then record it. There's no question it's boring and dull work. But from the information gathering foundation will develop a retirement plan built on accurate data and information.

Flip over to the end of the book and review the data form. We have purposely left it blank so you can use this as a data-gathering packet for yourself. I urge you not to skip any area. Take your time and fill it out completely. There may be areas you are not sure of so it can be helpful to talk to a professional (i.e., your financial planner, accountant or attorney).

As an example, as you are reviewing your automobile and home owner's policies call your agent and ask him to do an audit of your contracts. While he is doing the audit, ask him to make recommendations on any gaps in your coverage or areas where you may save premium dollars. Do the same with your life insurance coverage. Call your agent, or various agents, and requests the audit to get updated values of the cash value, death benefit, premium payments, and the beneficiaries for each policy.

Beneficiaries are especially important. Two weeks ago a new client and his wife were in our office. They are from a town 30 miles outside of Tulsa and had hired us to complete a comprehensive financial plan. They own two small businesses in their town and had accumulated a substantial amount of real estate. This was the second marriage for both of them. Guess who was listed as beneficiary on one of his life insurance policies? If you guessed the first wife, who he had been divorced from for over 10 years, you are correct! I have seen incorrect beneficiaries more times than you can imagine.

Am I making the sale to you on gathering all the information? The hardest part is gathering the data the first time, but once you get it is yours for ever. The information can be adjusted every year or so without much hassle because things won't change a lot year by year.

Goal setting

As I sat across from the table from Ted and Ruth, that cold day last January, I ask, "How much will you need to live on during your retirement years?" Ted, the engineer that he was, had that answer ready. "We will need 60% of our current income," he said. I turned and looked at Ruth and said, "Ruth how do you feel about that number?" Ruth was a little hesitant to answer because Ted was always so sure of himself and his calculations. Finally she said, "I don't think that's going to be enough. The kids live in different states and we will want to see them more often once we are retired. Ted really doesn't know how much it cost me to keep the house going smoothly and there are a lot of things he doesn't keep track of."

As a financial planner, with 50 years of experience, I must say Ruth is probably more in line with the truth than Ted. The studies I have seen suggest that most families need 75% to 100% of their pre-retirement income. Let me qualify that statement. At retirement, there are some expenses that will drop off so they can be subtracted from the current gross income. After retirement you will not be contributing to these items:

- 401(k) or IRA.
- Social Security taxes (7.65%)

Therefore, you can deduct these from your gross income. Let's assume that Ted's gross income is $150,000 per year. If his 401(k) contribution is 10% ($15,000) and his Social Security tax is 7.65% ($8,950) then his current income before tax is $126,050.

$150,000 Current Gross Salary
-$ 15,000 401k Contribution
-$ 8,950 Social Security Tax
$ 126,050 Current Spendable before tax

If everything else remains the same Ted and Ruth could maintain their same lifestyle and spending patterns on $126,050 per year (before income taxes). That is 82% of their current gross income. Ted may be right that they could live on only $90,000 (60% of his current gross) but that would be quite an adjustment from a $126,050 they now have available before tax. It should be pointed out there are some other items which may be reduced at retirement. For instance their health insurance costs may go up or down depending on what he was currently paying at Sunoco. They also may have been saving a considerable amount of additional money besides his 401(k) contribution. At retirement that should not be necessary. What about the mortgage on their house. Would the house be paid off anytime after retirement? As you can see, determining what you might need at retirement takes some thoughtfulness.

My experience is most people need between 75% and 100% of their current spendable income during retirement (i.e. after deducting for Social Security and a 401(k) contribution). Ruth had a good point about traveling to see the children. There is a tendency to spend more during the early retirement years because of all the free time. You can now travel more, go to movies more often, go shopping more often, play golf or fish more, and see the kids more often. These are all fun things to do and they cost money.

A perfect example is a couple named Tommy and Julie. Tommy retired in 2004 after 32 years with a major manufacturer. Before retiring Tom he had approximately $60,000 of annual income. Most of their expenses were paid off, including their house, so they thought they could get by on $40,000 a year from their 401(k) retirement account. It has now been four years since Tommy retired. The company hired him back on a consulting basis, which allowed him to make $40,000 a year. That gave them a total income over the last four years of $80,000 per year ($20,000 higher than before retirement). Do you think any of the extra $20,000 has been saved? If you answered no than you won the prize. The truth is the American way is to spend all of what we make.

As a financial professional I have recommended two methods for retirees to estimate their income needs after retiring. The first, and preferable one, uses a cash flow worksheet which is part of data form (see appendix A). The first page covers the budget and expense items. Some people find it shocking when they list everything they are currently spending. Next comes the income and other assets. We allows for adjustments after retirement of those items paid off after retirement. The final page accounts for debt. The problem with the worksheet is it is time-consuming and tedious; however, accurate projection of income needs at retirement far outweigh the work involved.

The second method to estimate retirement income needs is what many call 'guesstimating'. That is the method that Ted used in our original meeting.

As you can imagine the method preferred by a great many people is the "guesstimating" because of its simplicity. The problem is it typically doesn't estimate what will really be needed and too often is on the low side of income needs.

Assumptions

As Ted and Ruth sat in my office a year ago he leaned back in his chair and reached over to take Ruth's hand. The engineer in him had slipped to the back of his mind and he was less confident now. Ted said, "Can you take the mystery out of projecting our retirement income needs?" I said, "Ted, our process is rather straightforward. First we gather information on you and Ruth. Second we help you calculate what your cash flow needs will be after retirement.

We discuss with you some basic assumptions to use in our analysis. And finally, we make a projection of what your needs will be and whether your assets and sources of income will be adequate to meet those needs. I asked, "Does that sound like a reasonable process?"

The assumptions part of this process involves information from several sources. First we have to understand Ted and Ruth's investment risk tolerance since this will have a great deal to do with how the money is invested. Risk tolerance is typically found by asking a series of questions which help determine the experience level of the investor and their comfort with stock market variations in value. Some people would use the term risk instead of variations. Perhaps they're correct, but my philosophy is that there is a difference in risk and variations in value. I will be explaining my position on risk and variations in value using the context of a diversified portfolio of mutual funds. I am not making this definition applied to individually owned, common stock holdings.

Assume we have two brothers who have an equal amount of money which will be invested. One brother chooses to open a Chinese restaurant in his neighborhood. He will invest the entire amount of cash and opens his restaurant to the general public. The second brother goes in a different route. He divides his money between seven different mutual funds which own stocks and bonds invested in great American companies. (As a side note, there are many reasons for diversification. One is from the Bible. I believe the Bible is one of the best sources of principles to live by.

Below is a scripture from Ecclesiastics, "Divide Your Portion between seven, no eight, for no one knows what evil may befall the World". The funds are not only managed by professional money managers, but they also invest in very different type companies. For example, the money may be divided between large growth companies, large value companies, small growth and value, midsize growth and value, international, real estate, and bonds.

Time marches on and two years have gone by when we checked back in on our brothers. What might the results be? The first brother may have done well or may be out of business. If he is out of business, most likely he has lost his entire investment. Bummer!

11

The second brother may have an account that has gone up or down in value, depending on the economy, world events, and the equity market; however, there has never been a time in U.S. history when all accounts have gone to zero (Stocks for the Long Run, Jeremy Siegel). My point is that there is a difference between the risk of an investment going to zero (i.e., like the Chinese restaurant) and variation in value.

It is a good idea to redo your risk tolerance questionnaire as you enter the retirement phase of your life. During the working years of your life you are in what many call the accumulation phase. Your goals and objectives are much different in the accumulation phase than in the distribution phase (the distribution phase is that part of your life when the focus has changed from accumulating more assets to the distribution of those assets over your lifetime). During the accumulation phase you had time to let your money come back if there is a decline in the stock market. Upon entering the distribution phase you may not have time for your portfolio to rebound. Now you are liquidating – cashing in – your assets and it doesn't sit well if the stock market is down.

In our practice we divide risk tolerance profiles into six categories.

- **Profile I** is the most conservative or defensive profile. It consists normally of 80% bonds and 20% diversified stocks.
- **Profile 2** consists of 60% bonds and 40% diversified stocks.
- **Profile 3** consists of 40% bonds and 60% diversified stocks.
- **Profile 4** consists of 25% bonds and 75% diversified stocks.
- **Profile 5** consists of 15% bonds and 75% diversified stocks.
- **Profile 6** consists of 10% bonds and 90% diversified stocks.

The answers to a risk tolerance questionnaire plus a person's past 'estment experience helps determine the risk profile selected for Ted Ruth. It is not unusual for a person to be a Profile 4 or 5 during accumulation period. When they move into retirement, the \ution phase of their life, they may reposition their investments to \e 3 or 2. This change typically means less variation in their \ values.

By determining the profile which is appropriate we can then began making earnings assumptions for the investment portfolio. What should you assume your investments will earn? That is a question for the ages. Our position, as financial planners, is you should assume a conservative rate of return. Most in our profession would agree that 4% to 6% will be in the reasonable area. Later in this chapter I will discuss a study done by Fidelity Investments of retiree withdrawal rates and their suggestion of the most prudent withdrawal amount.

So far, in our assumptions, we have agreed upon a risk tolerance for Ted and Ruth, and the rate of return on their investments. There is one more important assumption which is what should we assume inflation will be going forward. Once again, Ted would like to have a concrete number so that he could apply his geometric formulas. Problem is inflation has not been a static number. Since 1930 it has gone from a low of 0% to a high of 13%.

I said, "Ted let's look at inflation from a distant point of view. If we go back to 1930 inflation has averaged approximately 3.1%*. If we only go to 1970 you will find that inflation is averaged approximately 4.6%. Source: JP Morgan, Guide to the Markets. Most likely over your lifetime inflation will be somewhere between those two numbers. What would you prefer to use? If you ask me my personal opinion, on what is a proper number to use, I use 3.0% in my own planning."

Financial independence

We all dream and plan for financial independence. But what does that actually mean and how do you calculate when you have achieved financial independence? In our practice we believe there is a number that represents a family's financial independence. In other words, having enough assets so the income provided by those assets, together with social security and pension benefits, will be sufficient to maintain their lifestyle for as long as they both live. We call this amount of asset the **'financial independence number'**. So you might say it is a number. If your assets are below your **"financial independence number"** you run the risk of running out of income and assets. If your assets are above the number there is a good likelihood you will have sufficient income for lifetime and even be able to pass on money to the next generation. Everything we've talked about to this point is used to determine the number for any given family to be financially independent.

Stress testing

It's not enough, in our opinion, to just make some assumptions, grab onto a number and think we are guaranteed financial independence. Stress testing our assumptions is prudent. Remember we are dealing with Ted and Ruth potentially living another 30 years. Any number of things can change during that time... rates of return will go up as well as down. Inflation can skyrocket. With this in mind I asked Ted, "since you have a background in engineering would you build a structure which has to survive the elements without having some method of testing how the structure stood up under stress?" Ted answered rather confidently, "of course I wouldn't. As a professional engineer I am required to test all of our assumptions."

Sitting across the table from Ted and Ruth I reached behind me and pulled from my credenza an example of the stress testing we do of our financial plans. Now we were getting into an area Ted could feel comfortable with. The "it's a mystery to me" was being washed out of Ted's mind and replaced by a solid, documented case of a financial retirement plan providing Ted and Ruth comfort and peace of mind.

You may be wondering how to stress test financial assumptions in a retirement plan? I must admit it is not easy and people much, much smarter than I am have developed such tools and techniques. We use several sophisticated retirement software programs. They take into consideration the variables we have talked about... the client's data, their income goals and objectives, the assumed rates of return, and inflation. One of these programs is so sophisticated it has the ability to analyze the client's current investment portfolio and give the average rate of return it would have earned since 1970. Once the retirement plan has been developed our feelings are it should be 'stressed tested' in several different ways. When you are 78 years old is not the time to find out your plan is running short of money...being a greeter at a Wal-Mart store is not an alternative we want to chose!

In the financial services industry there are several methods to test a retirement plan's ability to survive during difficult times. I will cover three of the more common ones. Please understand these are quite complicated and take sophisticated computer programs to run the calculations.

The first, and probably, most frequently used method applies historical average rates of return from a specified period (i.e. perhaps 1970). This information is fed into the computer along with the client data and income assumptions. Basically the computer calculates what the assets available, together with other sources of income (i.e., such as Social Security and pension income), invested at the historical average rates of return, will provide for the income needs of the retirees. Many plans end with this calculation. In our opinion you need to go much deeper. Average rates of return can be very misleading and may not provide a true picture of the plans results. For instance, the people who retired in 1972 were immediately affected by the stock market decline of 40% in 1973 to 1974. An average return of 9.5% from the S&P 500 from 1970 to 2007 didn't mean much to those people since their account had already declined by approximately 40% in just their first two years.

In our opinion, a retiree should have one or more additional test run. Most financial planners agree these tests should be completed. The second stress test of the retirement plan calculations is called the 'historical returns'. Remember in the test above we use the average returns from 1970. The second test uses the actual historical returns on a five-year rolling average. This takes into consideration short periods of time when there might have been substantial decreases in the stock market. This test will show weaknesses if there is a likelihood your account will run out of money. Please understand these historical periods may not recur in our lifetime, but it is a good idea to review these calculations to see how well your retirement plan would stand up if such a period reoccurred.

The third stress test assumes retiring at various historical times, beginning in 1925. In other words, it takes your own account together with your assumptions and assumed that you retired in 1925 and every five years thereafter. Each calculation is run as though you retired in a specific year to see whether your plan would have survived those various time periods. For instance, assume you retired in 1930 during the middle of the Depression... how would your account have performed. It's surprising at looking at these numbers to see how varied the results can be.

The final stress test is the Monte Carlo simulation. As you know, Monte Carlo is a Mecca for gaming. Monte Carlo simulation stress test applies 'probabilities' to determine whether your account may or may not perform as you would like. The computer programmers use all of the historical events which have affected the financial markets since 1900 and then randomly apply it to your particular portfolio and income needs. The result is a graph showing the probability your plan will or will not succeed over your lifetime.

Risk factors to your retirement plan

Retirees are approaching retirement very differently from those of previous generations. Consider these facts baby boomers are facing:

- many people are retiring earlier and having higher expectations about their retirement years
- with our increasing lifespan, spending 30 years or more in retirement is a realistic possibility 1 (Social Security Administration, Office of Policy, Income of the Ages chart book 2002, issued September 2004)
- only 25% of families include a member covered by a traditional pension plan or a retiree health-care plan 2 (Alicia Munnell and Annika Sunden, Coming up Short: the Challenge of 401(k) Plans, January 2004

A year has passed since my initial meeting with Ted and Ruth. They are more relaxed and positive about their future in retirement. After developing the retirement analysis for Ted and Ruth (with the stress test mentioned earlier), the engineer in Ted took over and he became more confident the numbers were accurate and could work out for a comfortable and secure retirement. It must have been close to six months after our original meeting when Ted said to me, "Skip, I can't tell you how much this step-by-step retirement process has meant to Ruth and I. When we first met you, there was a lot of apprehension and confusion about being able to retire comfortably... about not running out of money. I wasn't kidding when I said, 'It's a mystery'. And then, during our second meeting when you outlined the five key risks we would face in retirement, Ruth and I almost decided to put retirement on hold. Thanks for being patient with us. Going through the entire process of developing a retirement plan has given us a new comfort."

Five Key Risk Retirees Face

I my opinion the 'five key risk' that Ted spoke of should be integrated into every retirement plan. They can be devastating to any person retiring. If you are reading this for the first time please jot them down and make a point to understand how they affect you. (America's life time income challenge. Fidelity Investments White Paper)

1) **Longevity**
2) **Health-Care Expenses**
3) **Inflation**
4) **Asset allocation**
5) **Excess withdrawals**

Longevity... Challenge: many people underestimate their life span and therefore risk outliving assets

Most people think in terms of life expectancy. But by definition, half of the population will live longer than their life expectancy and half will live shorter. Retirees can drastically underestimate how long their savings must provide for them.

19 years ago I attended a conference at which an actuary from the Social Security Administration spoke. He suggested financial

17

professionals should start assuming our clients will live to age 90. I thought he made a solid point. I started talking to many of my clients about using age 90 as their life expectancy, but most of them would not agree. Over the years, people are now more acceptable to using 90 as life expectancy. Study the chart below and come to your own conclusion.

Retirees Should Plan for Living Longer Than They Think

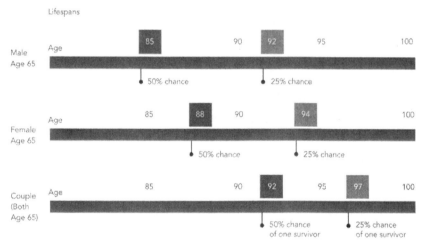

Retirees should plan for longer life expectancies due to increasing longevity

Source: Annuity 2000 Mortality Table; Society of Actuaries. Figures assume a person is in good health.

Sources: Annuity 2000 Mortality Table; Society of Actuaries

Health care expenses... Challenge: Health care cost when added to inadequate health care coverage may bring hardship to a retirement plan

Longer life spans, declining employer sponsored medical coverage, rising medical costs, possible shortfalls ahead for Medicare all add up to make health care expenses a challenge for retirees.

We are estimating retirees may need to fund a considerable portion of their own health care expenses not covered by Medicare. Also most people do not consider the rising cost of Medicare and Medicare supplement policy premiums. These rise at a faster rate than inflation and over the last 10 years the cost has risen at a rate of 7% per year. They may go up annually and become quite substantial. In addition, there are the insurance deductibles, over counter drugs, co-pays, etc. (source: Fidelity Employer Service Company; Health and Welfare Consulting;) A recent congressional report estimates medical expenses in United States will increase by 200% by 2022. A 2009 study by Fidelity Employer Service Company estimates a couple retiring today at age 65 will need current savings of at least $240,000 to supplement Medicare, Medicare premium increases, and their out of pocket health care cost during retirement. With more pressure put on the government because of its high debt, many of costs may be passed on to the individual.

These estimates do not include the possibility of long-term care needed by the retirees. The average cost in United States in 2007 for long-term care ranged from $45,589 to $157,113 per year depending on the region and quality level of care. These are significant amounts of money. When you consider that roughly half of those people age 65 today will be admitted to a nursing home at some point in their lives, it becomes clear how important it is to ensure you can cover these expenses. (Source: Genworth Financial, 2007 cost of care survey, March 2007, page 26 through 29)

Inflation...the hidden demon so easy to ignore

Inflation is a household word. For the baby boomers it is reality and expected. While a person is working inflation was somewhat benign since their incomes would normally follow it. This is not true at retirement because their paycheck has stopped and inflation chips away at retirement income in two ways:

- increasing the future cost of goods and services
- potentially eroding the value of assets set aside to meet those costs

I have a wonderful example of the ravages of inflation. In 1967 my wife, Carol and I bought our first house. Two of our children were born there. It was a three-bedroom brick home with a formal living room and family room...a nice home in middle income America. Recently we found the old box in the attic with stored checks from our first winter in our home. Our natural gas bill for the month of December 1967 was $12. For the month of January 1968 it was $17. (By the way our home was heated with natural gas) If we were to retire in that same house today how much do you think our natural gas bill would be in the those same months of the winter? Ten times higher is probably not out of line. If a retirees income had not increase along the way their life style/standard of living will have gone down substantially...the devastating effects of inflation.

The effect of inflation on purchasing power

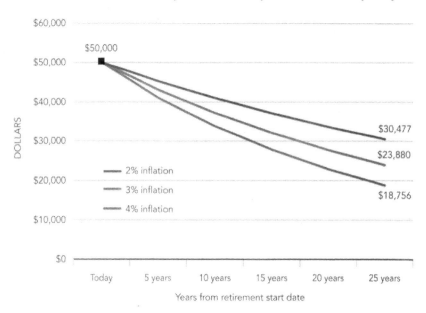

The effect of inflation on purchasing power

Even at a low inflation rate of 2%, in 25 years $50,000 will buy as much as $30,477 buys today.

All numbers were calculated based on hypothetical rates of inflation of 2%, 3%, and 4% (historical average from 1926 to 2009 was 3%) to show the effects of inflation over time; actual inflation rates

Asset allocation Risk...don't put all your eggs in one basket

As retirement approaches many people get concerned about losing their money in stocks. They avoid the stock of great American companies and focus on CDs and fixed income investments. Statistics show losing the long term growth potential of stock in great American companies may actually increase, not decrease, the risk of outliving their money. Source: Fidelity Investments, American's Lifetime Income Challenge, page 10

There is no question market risk comes with investing. We certainly can't control what the stock market behaves like; however, we do have choices in how we invest which can help manage the long term effects of owning stock in great American companies. Specifically, I'm speaking of asset allocation, which strives to strike a balance between stocks, bonds and short-term investments.

As a planner I've been advised and coached on avoiding the extremes. Being too aggressive in a portfolio can increase your vulnerability to market fluctuations. At the same time a portfolio that is too conservative may not outpace inflation, thereby increasing the risk you will dip into you principle which may cause a person to outlive their assets (asset allocation does not ensure a profit or a guarantee against a loss). The challenge for retirees with a portfolio overly concentrated in CD and bond investments expose themselves to a greater risk of outliving their assets since they may have to invade their principle. On the other, hand the retiree must be cautioned against owning too high a percentage of the assets in stock since there is a high potential for a decline in account value. It is a difficult balancing act. As the chart below shows a balanced approach is prudent. (Refer back to page 15 for various asset allocation profiles)

Stocks should be part of a retirement portfolio...Fidelity white paper

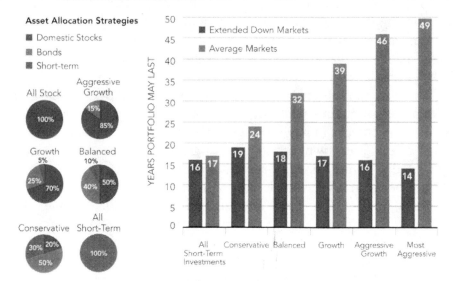

Stocks should be part of a retirement portfolio

How long your money may last depends on your asset allocation and the long-term performance of the market. Consider, for example, a 6% withdrawal rate strategy.

Source: Fidelity Investments. Average rates of return for stocks, bonds, short-term investments, and inflation are based on the risk premium approach. Actual rates of return may be more or less. The chart is for illustrative purposes only and is not indicative of any investment. Past performance is no guarantee of future results.

Source: Fidelity Investments, America's lifetime income challenge, page 10

Withdrawal Risk...challenge: higher withdrawal rates can derail your plan no matter what your asset mix

At the time you retire the amount you withdrawal per month is largely in your control. The chart below shows how the amount withdrawn can have a dramatic effect on how long your money will last.

During the bull market of the 1980s and 1990s, the S&P 500 grew at over 15% per year. With these high rates of return, people became overly optimistic in their withdrawal rates. Retirees believed they could withdraw 7%, 8%, or even more per year, believing they could count on rising stock prices to keep the total value of their investments unchanged or even growing. In 2000 through 2002 we had a bear market followed by another bear market in 2008. These bear market declines point out the high withdrawal fallacy.

The chart below shows how different withdrawal rates may affect the length of time a pool of assets will last. The chart takes a balanced portfolio (i.e., 50% stocks, 40% bonds, and 10% short term bonds) of $500,000 and tracks it over the period from 1972 to 2008 assuming a 3% inflation adjusted withdrawal rate. We specifically picked 1972 as a year of retirement since it was the beginning of a two-year decline in the stock market. From this chart it is alarming to see a couple, both age 65, would have run out of money at age 88 if the had withdrawn 5%, adjusted upward for inflation each year.

Prudent withdrawal rates can extend the life of a portfolio

if you had retired in 1972 with $500,000

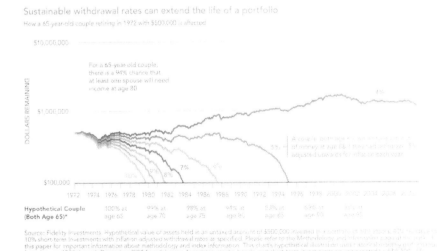

Challenge: withdrawal rates much above 4%, especially in the early years of retirement, may increase the likelihood you will deplete your assets prematurely

Summary

Developing a retirement plan can be a daunting process, but the good news is you do not have to go it alone. There are a number of excellent financial advisors who are well equipped to help you with this process and make it smooth and easier. These are the items we have covered so far in preparing to get your retirement plan and your entire 'financial house in order'.

- Identify your income needs in retirement
  - o our goal is to create a realistic budget based on your desired lifestyle and your assets available
- all sources of income should be considered
  - o we looked over all sources of income and assets that will help fund your retirement
- allocate your investment portfolio
  - o chose investments to meet growth and income needs. You will need to take into account factors such as withdrawal rates, age, and risk tolerance.
- Monitor your plan regularly
  - o review your plan yearly. Be willing and ready to adjust your plan as your life changes in retirement or as your investments change

Chapter 3
Financial Road Map

I arrived at the office at 8:45 A.M. My first appointment is typically scheduled a little after nine o'clock so my plan has been to get to the office 15 minutes early, review my schedule, eat a bowl of oatmeal and blue berries, and sip on some hot green tea. After booting up my computer and logging onto my schedule, I notice the first appointment is with Ted and Ruth Dunleavy. The file is on my desk and as I look over the notes on the front cover I leaned back in my chair and though about our first appointment. Wow, has it been 12 months since the first meeting with the Dunleavy's? Our files are well organized and chronologically list all the steps taken over this last year. They have accomplished a great deal.

I crack a small grin as I read the note from the first meeting…those famous words from Ted during our first meeting…"retirement planning is a mystery." Like the engineer he is, Ted has gotten up to speed quickly with the work we have done. The systematic thoroughness of our retirement plan together with the stress testing has put his mind at ease about their being able to retire comfortably without worrying about running out of money. The 'mystery' has been put to rest and in its place is a documented, well thought out retirement strategy for Ted and Ruth.

What do we talk about today at our meeting? Of course we can review their investment portfolio and discuss any tweaking to be done to align it with what's going on in the economy.

I decide we will only spend a few moments on the accounts. Today Ted and Ruth are going to be introduced to 'The Financial Roadmap'. You see they thought once we develop their retirement strategy all of the planning was complete. How wrong they were. A retirement plan was a big step in the right direction, but it certainly didn't address all of the many complicated areas of our lives while living in the 21st century.

Have you ever woken in the middle of the night wondering about something financial? Perhaps you have thought, "Did I give my accountant that extra tax deduction?" Or maybe it was, "our attorney set up our trust, have I changed my beneficiaries to the trust?" Or, "I better get to the attorney before our trip to Europe and change our will". You and I could go on and on about questions we have involving our complicated financial lives. There are dozens of big and little details which need to be handled. *Have you done them all?* *Do you even know what they all are?* This is an area where the old saying **"they don't know what they don't know"** is so very true.

Introduction to the Financial Roadmap

You have just come across the reason for this book. After several decades of reviewing retirement and financial plans, I found no organized, written process for people to address all of these issues and questions. The idea of putting down a systematized schedule for accomplishing this was given to me by Bob Simpson of Toronto, Canada. He is a professional coach who helped analyze my financial planning practice so it ran more effectively. During one of our coaching calls Bob said, "Skip, you would be well served to develop a system to help your clients address all of the financial concerns that they face in their life." He is right…there is no written system that I know of designed to help people accomplish such a goal. So if this is the pioneering system which helps tie it all together, then I guess we are part of this pioneering process.

It's not that these things have not been addressed in the past, because they have. They have been addressed individually by the various professions. Your insurance agent address insurance items. Your attorney addressed wills and trust documents. Your accountant addressed the tax issues. The financial planner worked on accumulating and protecting you assets.

There's nothing wrong with having a number of advisors, but what happens if you leave one or two of these people out of the process? What happens if they don't address everything in a comprehensive fashion? May I share with you a real life example. Remember the couple I mention that had been married 10 years and yet we found out his first wife was still named as a beneficiary on one of his life insurance policies? Was the problem he had not talked with an insurance person in the last 10 years...or met an attorney who is an expert in beneficiary designations?

No! This man and his wife own two businesses and have solid professional advisors. He has purchased life insurance in the last 10 years and has worked with his attorney a number of times. Why wasn't this error caught? Don't you think that $500,000 in death benefit being paid to the wrong person is significant? Perhaps it's because our processes do not reward checking on items as in this example. The insurance agent gets paid for selling new policies...any attorney gets paid for reviewing and drawing new wills and trust. Either one of these professionals may never ask to review old insurance policies.

You have the genesis of the 'financial roadmap'. We've labeled it **"Roadmap to get your financial house in order"**. Its purpose is to make certain nothing of a financial nature is left unaddressed.

The Road Map

As your trusted Advisor, our team goes the extra mile with a road map to achieving your financial goals and helps you stay on-track for the long-term. This is an ongoing process.

About 9:30 a.m. in the morning Karen, our managing partner, called and said Ted and Ruth had arrived. She got them coffee, cream no sugar, and brought them back to my office. After a few pleasantries I said to Ted and Ruth, "it has been over a year since we started the journey of developing your retirement strategy. I want to continue the journey today with a new tool. I call it a financial roadmap. It is designed to 'get your financial house in order'. It is a roadmap of our agenda over the next several years. Since we meet on a regular basis I've developed a theme for each of those meetings. Of course we will review the investments each time, but that will not be the main focus of our meetings. The main focus will be a particular theme/topic. This is an outline of those meetings (review the roadmap diagram and notice each meeting will cover a new topic).

As you can see we have already covered the first two sessions dealing with retirement planning. The rest of our themes will deal with the other areas of your financial life. The goal is to make certain nothing is left to chance. Today we will be discussing income and estate taxes. At our next meeting we will review all forms of your insurance and confirming both primary and contingent beneficiaries on life insurance policies, your 401k plan and IRA's. During a subsequent meeting we will review your asset allocation and update your risk tolerance to confirm your portfolio is still appropriate. A future meeting will cover your wills, trust, legacy plans, life time gifts, and methods of passing on assets...very personal topics which we many times avoid discussing because of their sensitive nature. We will complete the 'Financial Road Map' with a family meeting. This applies more to our families with older children since it deals with legacy planning, income and lump sum distributions, and why those decisions were made. It might even involve having the grandchildren in attendance so grandma and granddad can share family history and their views on living a successful life. How does that sound to you?"

This time Ruth was first to speak. She said, "some of the topics you mention are not important to me at this time; however, several items on the 'roadmap' have concerned me for a long time. I have not known where to turn for help or how to solve the problem, so I am looking forward to going through the 'roadmap'.

Chapter 4
Tax Saving Information...It's Your Money!

I followed up on the Ruth's comment by saying, "As we begin your journey through the financial roadmap let me point out I am not an accountant. My purpose in talking with you about this part of the "get your house in order" is simply to review some of the basic tax areas that will affect the two of you over your lifetime. My purpose is simply to provide an overview. I will not be giving you tax advice or even getting into many of the fine points of the tax law. That is a responsibility of your tax planner. Your responsibilities will be to get proper accounting and legal advice on any of the items you want to explore in more detail. Since we manage your investments we want to make sure you have a basic understanding of the things which might help reduce the tax impact on you."

"Your assets, from a taxable viewpoint, can be broadly divided into three categories:

- o taxable savings or investments
- o tax-deferred savings or investments
- o tax-free savings or investments

About this time somebody might comment, "I would like all of mine to be tax-free". The interesting fact is each category has an important role to play. All categories have advantages and disadvantages. As a planner your individual situation and your needs will determine which category should contain varying amounts of your savings or investments.

Taxable savings and investments

Taxable assets and savings simply mean these funds are owned in such a way the interest or earnings are taxed each year when you file your income tax return. The ownership method is typically in the name of the owner and/or joint tendency with the spouse or other family member. These are typically divided by the category of savings or investment. There are three broad categories:

Guaranteed Accounts savings accounts, checking accounts, certificates of deposit, etc. these instruments are may be ensured by the FDIC. The earnings in these accounts are taxed at the end of the year. Both you and the federal and state government received a notice of how much interest you have earned off of your accounts. You pay ordinary income tax in the year you receive the earnings. We will look at a tax table, in a few pages, which will illustrate how these earnings most likely will be taxed at your highest tax bracket.

Taxable Bonds/Debt Instruments…The earnings in these accounts are taxed at the end of the year. Both you, the federal and state government received a notice of how much interest you have earned off of your accounts. You pay ordinary income tax in the year you receive the earnings.

Bond and debt instruments referred to the same type account. Instead of depositing the money in the bank you are loaning it typically to a government agency or a corporation. In the simplest form bonds are like an IOU. Interest is paid to the bondholder until the bond matures and the principle is repaid. Should the bond appreciate in value and then be sold, any appreciation (not interest) will be taxes at capital gains rates.

Bonds are normally considered safer than stock investments; however, bonds may be exposed to several risk. First, bonds are subject to interest rate risk. The value of the bond may decrease should interest go up. Second, bonds are subject to default if the issuer of the bond falls on hard times (i.e., for example, a bond issued by a corporation that goes into bankruptcy).

Tax free Municipal bonds

These are bonds issued by state and city governments (also some unincorporated territories of the US Government such as Puerto Rico). The income received from these bonds are free from Federal income tax. If the bonds were issued from the state where the bond holder resides the income is also income tax free from that state (i.e., these are referred to as double exempt). Should the bond appreciate in value and then be sold, any appreciation (not interest) will be taxes at capital gains rates. These bonds are subject to the same risk of the taxable bonds discussed above (i.e., the risk of default only applies if the governmental agency gets into financial trouble).

Equities... individual stocks, mutual funds invested in common stocks, or individually owned companies. The earnings on these equity investments are taxed in various manners. Individual stocks and mutual funds may pay dividends which are taxed at rates determined by an individual's tax rate on earned income. Dividends qualify for the 0% rate (tax free) if you fall within the 10% or 15% tax brackets. Dividends qualify for the 15% rate if you fall within next higher tax brackets, and 20% if you are in the highest tax bracket (39.6%). There are exceptions, so see IRS Publication 550 for more information.

If the stock or mutual funds are sold during the calendar year the gain is taxed at capital gains rates. Gains can be classified as short term gains or long term gains. Gains on securities held less than 12 months are taxed at the Federal level at ordinary income tax rates. Long term gains are taxed for Federal tax at capital gains rates.

This brings up an interesting potential investment opportunity from a taxable point of view. An individual may buy what appears to be a taxable investment such as a growth stock which does not pay dividends or raw land that provides no rental income. In this case these two investments may actually act as a tax-deferred investment since no dividends are earned, there would be no tax due until the property or stock was sold. For example, back in the 1980s Wal-Mart stock paid no dividend yet grew at a substantial rate. That meant that a person who own Wal-Mart stock from 1980 to 1990 might have had a substantial gain in the stock value each year, but paid no tax until the stock was sold. If they own the stock today they would pay capital gains tax on the gain. The same would be true of a piece of land that provides no rental income. The land might grow in value from $10,000 to $50,000 with no income tax being levied until the day the property sells. At the time of sale there would be a capital gains tax due.

Tax-deferred savings and investments

The tax-deferred category can be a very powerful category since the taxes are deferred until some future date. As above, in the taxable area, the tax-deferred area can own the account as a guaranteed account such as CDs or savings. The account can also be held in the bond/debt category as well as the equity category.

Most of the money is classified as tax-deferred gets its tax-deferred status from the federal government. Financial advisors and accountants have a special name for most of this money. It may be called 'qualified money'. The federal government has set up several rules to allow people to set money aside for their future use. The money set aside grows tax-deferred until it is withdrawn, typically at retirement age. In certain qualified accounts the money is also tax deductible from the person's income in the year earned. This is true for both state and federal income taxes.

Qualified accounts

Qualified accounts come in a number of different federally endorsed plans. The government is encouraging people to set aside money perhaps for their own retirement or children's education. The government is allowing the people to set aside the money and avoid paying current income taxes. They may also receive an income tax deduction in the year the contribution is made. Several accounts qualify in this area: pension plans, 401(k) plans, simplified employee pension plans (SEP-IRA), traditional IRA, simple IRA, 403 b plans, and 457 plans. Many times the contributions for these plans are withheld from the persons pay check. There is typically a trigger date when the funds must be withdrawn from the tax sheltered account. Some of these qualified plans will receive contributions both from the employer and the employee. The contributions are typically deductible and non-taxable as ordinary income until they are withdrawn.

Money accumulated in a tax-deferred account over time can provide substantially more value at retirement. For instance, assume an employee is accumulating money in a tax-deferred account and earning an average of 7% per year. The employee contributes $2000 a year and pays no income tax. If the account grows by 7% over a 30 year period that would accumulate to $202,146. This example does not include the benefit of a tax deduction. The illustration is only the tax deferral.

If the same employee contributed $2000 per year into a taxable account earning 7% he or she would have to pay income taxed each year on the 7%. Assuming they are in a 25% state and federal tax bracket they would lose approximately 1.75% of their interest earnings each year to the tax man (i.e. the state and federal government). Their average return, after taxes, would be 5.25% over the same 30 year. The account would grow, after taxes, to $146,008. The tax savings, as you can see can be substantial.

Non-qualified accounts

Nonqualified accounts also have federal regulations providing guidelines on what qualifies for this tax-deferral. The 'nonqualified accounts' do not provide an upfront tax deduction each year as the contribution is made. They provide only tax deferral of the earnings. But we've seen that the tax deferral can be a big advantage when compared with a taxable account.

Two of the frequently used nonqualified accounts come under these headings: nonqualified deferred compensation plans and annuities.

The nonqualified deferred compensation plans are set up by both business and nonprofit organizations for the benefit of their employees. Under these arrangements the company can allow an employee to defer part of their current earnings. The employee pays no income tax on the current earnings or the accumulations in the investment. The employee deposits are held and invested by the employer. The employee is eligible to take the deferred compensation account typically at a specified time in the future. It may be taken either in a lump sum or as an income. The deferred compensation account are classified as an assets on the corporate balance sheet until the funds are withdrawn.

Nonqualified annuities are typically purchased by individuals who desire to set aside money on a tax-deferred basis. The earning accumulates tax deferred. Typically, the money is withdrawn at retirement time. The benefit, of course is the fact the money grows on a tax-deferred basis. Annuities are purchased from insurance companies.

All of these tax-deferred accounts can be invested in the guaranteed accounts, bond accounts or equity accounts.

Tax-deferred accounts, whether qualified or nonqualified, have some general characteristics. These are rules and regulations established by the Internal Revenue Service. One of the main requirements is that the money be held in these account until age 59 1/2. The purpose of these accounts is to encourage people to provide additional money for their own retirement (hence the age 59 1/2 limit for penalty free withdrawal). An individual can delay withdrawal of the monies on qualified plans until age 70 ½. At 70 ½ the individual is required to begin Minimum Required Distributions from their account (MRD does not apply to non qualified annuities). There are exceptions for withdrawals before age 59 1/2. These rules are covered under section 72T of the Internal Revenue Code. They are somewhat involved and out of the scope of this discussion. I would simply advise you to talk with your accountant or financial advisors to make any of these calculations.

Tax-free accounts

As you can imagine these have an especially attractive ring to them. The old saying there are only two things certain in life, taxes and death. So you can imagine any type of tax-free account would be welcomed by everyone. As you can also imagine the government's not too excited about letting us, their citizens, accumulate money and avoid paying income taxes. There are not a lot of options in this category (we have already discussed tax free municipal bonds). Like anything else, there are rules and regulations which must be followed in order to make certain the money grows and comes out income tax-free.

First, let's talk about tax free categories:

Roth IRA... the federal government allows you to set aside money in a Roth IRA if you meet certain requirements. If you are single and your adjusted gross income is over $112,000 you probably are not going to be eligible to contribute to a Roth IRA. If you are married and filing a joint return you are not eligible if your adjusted gross income exceeds $178,000. Actually, there is a phased out for both the single and the married taxpayer, but it doesn't give you much ability to contribute to a Roth if you are exceeding the limits I mentioned. Also keep in mind the tax rules change as years go by so check with your advisor or accountant to make sure the rules you are learning are the current ones. If you qualify you can contribute $5,000 per person to the Roth IRA. You can not contribute both to a traditional IRA and a Roth IRA over the $5,000 limit. There is a $1000 catch-up provision for people over age 50. A person over age 50 can contribute an additional $1000 per year. The Roth does not provide an income tax deduction when the money is deposited, but the money grows tax-deferred. At withdraw the money comes out income tax-free.

Here's a great idea for your children or grandchildren. Make a gift to them of a Roth IRA. Here's an example of how this can provide a great benefit. I contributed to the Roth, for each of my three sons. Assume they have a total of $10,000 accumulated in their Roth by the time they reach age 25. Further assume the $10,000 grows at the rate of 8% a year (using one of the many mutual funds that are available). The money could grow tax-deferred for the next 40 years assuming the kids don't invade the account (I've threaten them if they did). $10,000, if it grew at 8%, could be worth $217,000 by the time they reach age 65. If the account continues to earn 8% interest they will be able to receive $17,379 per year and pay absolutely no income taxes. Should they live another 20 years and continue to receive that income they will have received $347,000 in income without paying any income tax. Assuming they have not spent the principle when they die their children or grandchildren will receive a $217,000 from the principal originally accumulated... **wow!!** How's that for an idea as a benefit to your children. The Roth works also for mom and dad, so don't forget to do one for yourself if you're eligible.

Tax-free municipal bonds... tax-free municipal bonds have been around forever (that is a little bit of a stretch, but a long time). I mentioned these a few pages ago...this will go into more detail. Tax free bonds are issued by state and city governments (for instance, if your city is having a school bond issued than you have an example of a tax-free bond). Typically the interest rate on tax-free bonds may be lower than on other forms of bonds of a similar duration (i.e., corporate or US Government bonds); however, they may be a very good alternative for some of your conservative money. Especially for those in a high tax bracket.

The bonds are free of federal income taxes in all situations. If the bond is issued by the state or a city from the state that you live in, the bonds will also be free from state income taxes. We call these doubly exempt bonds.

529 educational plans... 529 plans allow mom or dad, grandpa or grandma, or anyone else to set aside money for higher education and not pay income tax on the money's growth. As with our tax-deferred accounts you can use guaranteed accounts, bond/or debt accounts, and equity accounts. The money going into the 529 Educational Plan is typically set up for a child or grandchild. The deposit can be made into a number of different investment accounts available throughout the United States. While in the account, the money grows tax-deferred and may be withdrawn tax free if use for higher education. When the child or grandchild is ready to enroll in higher education (after high school) the money can be withdrawn for many of the various expenses tied to higher education. Expenses falling within the guidelines of the federal government provide all of the gain on the account comes out income tax-free.

As an example, granddad puts aside $10,000 when his first grandson, Declan, is born. Grandpa put the money in a mutual fund and we will assume it has earned 8% a year until Declan graduates at age 18. Assuming an 8% rate of return, the account will have grown to $39,960. If the money is used for the expenses of Declan's higher education, grandpa can withdraw all of the money, pay the expenses and never pay income taxes on the $29,960 gain! Not a bad use of grandpa's money. If the money is not used for college but for grandpa's needs, (i.e., instead of giving it to Declan for college) grandpa will pay the ordinary income tax on the gain, plus a 10% penalty.

Coverdell Educational Saving Account

A Coverdell Education Savings Accounts can be established for a child under age 18 and used for elementary, secondary, or post-secondary education expenses. The account is funded with after-tax contributions, which may be invested in mutual fund accounts as well as bank saving accounts. Assets accumulate tax-deferred, and qualified withdrawals are free from federal income tax. Contribution amounts are subject to income limitations, with a maximum contribution of $2,000 a year.

Cash value life insurance

Cash value life insurance has some unique tax aspects that can allow, under the right circumstances, money to accumulate on the tax deferred basis and then be withdrawn on a tax-free basis. In order to accomplish this, you must be very careful to observe a proper design of the life insurance policy as well as proper handling. We all understand that life insurance is purchased for the insurance death benefit. Policies creating cash value have been around for a century and many of the tax laws that apply to them seem as though they're almost that old. The unique rules governing cash value life insurance can be very advantageous for the person who needs insurance and also wants to accumulate tax-free income.

Following are the four general tax rules that apply to cash value life insurance:

1) Cash value in a life insurance policy accumulates tax deferred (IRS code section 72)
2) Withdrawal of the cash value can be made income tax-free up to the cost basis of the policy. Life insurance is one of the few vehicles still taxed on the accounting principle of first in first out (FIFO). This means your contributions (i.e. premium payments) can be withdrawn from the policy income tax-free as they were the first dollars contributed and you are only withdrawing your contribution... you are not withdrawing your profit.
3) Policy loans against the policy cash value can be taken income tax-free. Loans have been permitted from insurance policies for perhaps one hundred years. Loans from a bank or credit union used to buy a house or an automobile are not taxed as ordinary income; therefore, using the same principal loans against your life insurance policy also are tax-free.
4) Policy death benefits paid at the death of the insured are income tax-free.

I think you'll agree these four items are fairly cut and dry. The beauty comes when they are all used in conjunction with a cash value policy. They allow the policy holder to accumulate money tax-deferred then take policy withdrawals (up to the cost basis) and then switch to policy loans. Up to this point, there has been no income tax paid on the benefits. The next key is the insurance policy must stay in effect until the death of the insured. Presto, the death benefits are paid income tax-free. To sum it up no taxes would be paid during the insured lifetime or at death.

In order for this concept to work it's very important that the plan be designed properly. In my estimation the policy needs to be designed to emphasize the cash value buildup and to deemphasize the death benefit. In that way you are allowed to build up the maximum cash value and keep the cost of the insurance to a minimum.

Home equity

Under current tax laws the value of your house can provide an attractive way to accumulate money on a tax-free basis. Recently the tax laws were changed so that an individual, as long as they live in their house for two of the last five years, could sell their house and realize up to $250,000 in profit and not have to pay any ordinary income or capital gains tax. For a couple this amount is $500,000 in profit. The law has not always been this way. Before the tax law change, any profit on your house was fully taxable... bummer! There was one exception. The exception applied to people over age 55 and could be used only once in a lifetime. It allowed a profit of up to $250,000 with no income tax being collected.

Applying what we've learned about taxable, tax-deferred and tax-free

Now that we have addressed the various taxable categories (taxable accounts, tax-deferred accounts, and tax-free accounts) you might be in a better position to make some intelligent decisions about the positioning of your funds. You can call it a repositioning strategy or perhaps a capital transfer strategy. These moves take study and good counsel. Remember this book is not designed to give you all the tax strategies that might apply to your situation. Its purpose is to open your mind to items that may benefit you and give you an example of how this might help you in your future planning.

Creativity can save you money

A simple repositioning strategy might save you a considerable amount of money over your lifetime. It involves transferring the earnings out of a taxable investment and placing them into a tax-deferred or tax-free investment. Let's use Ted and Ruth as an example. These are the assumptions. Bear with me as we set the scene using one of their children. Susie is 37 years old and has over $20,000 in her savings account (this represents five months of her income). In addition she has $30,000 in a taxable mutual fund she inherited from her grandfather. The dividends and capital gains on the fund have been reinvested and her plan is to continue to reinvest the money over her lifetime and use this money for retirement in 30 years.

Do the math with me; $30,000 in her mutual fund growing at 10% a year will generate approximately $3000 this year in capital gains and dividends. Assuming those are taxed at combined Oklahoma state and federal capital gains tax rate of 22% she will pay approximately $660 in capital gains taxes. We will assume when the taxes are due she will pay them out of her regular salary earnings and not liquidate any of the mutual funds (I find this is what the majority of people do). When Susie reaches age 65, assuming her account continues to grow at a rate of 10% (the average rate of the Standard & Poor's index*over the last 70 year (Source: JPMorgan, Guide to the Markets, 1Q/2014) her account will have reached a value of $523,000. Remember that is the way compounding works... pretty amazing! And that is assuming she makes no additional contributions. That's the good news; the bad news is her capital gains and dividends subject to tax the thirtieth year will be approximately $52000. The capital gains tax, assuming the rates are still at 22% will be $11,500... double bummer.

As a reminder this exercise is designed to give you a way to save money. Let's say we make one minor change. Instead of reinvesting the earnings back into the same mutual fund let's assume the earnings are withdrawn every year and money is contributed to a Roth IRA (you could also make a larger contribution to your 401(k) with the same dollars). The magic of following this suggestion is you freeze the income tax at the level of the first year because all of the dividends and growth are transferred each year into the Roth IRA. After 30 years, Susie will have two accounts... the original $30,000 that her granddad left her will still be worth $30,000 as a result of all of the earnings being transferred yearly into the Roth IRA account. Her Roth IRA account has a value of $490,000. Her taxes at the thirtieth year are still levied only on the $30,000 capital gain and dividends meaning the taxes are still $660 instead of the $11,500. Going forward, when Susie begins withdrawing from her Roth IRA account those dollars will come out totally income tax-free whereas the $523,000 in the original example would have taxes due of approximately $11,000 each year.

As I mentioned earlier it's important to get professional advice when you reposition assets. Questions need to be answered before monies are moved. For instance, will I need the growth or dividends that I'm transferring into my Roth? You should consider the tax penalties if you take the money out of the Roth before age 59 1/2.

Some other repositioning strategies could include these areas:

- transferred from savings into bonds or equities
- transfer from taxable accounts into tax-deferred or tax-free accounts
- transfer from parents to children's accounts (i.e. children may be in a lower or no tax bracket) if eventually the children are to use the money
- transfer from ordinary income tax rate items to capital gains tax rate items

Marginal tax rates versus average tax rates

As Ted and Ruth and I were reviewing these items on taxes I ask, "Ted, what is your marginal tax bracket?" (Remember Ted is the engineer and engineers know their numbers) Ted didn't hesitate a second, he shot back, "Skip, it is 18%." I replied, "Ted, I think that is your average tax rate. I want to know is what your marginal tax rate is." Engineers are so predictable and Ted was no exception. He didn't like being in the dark about something he thought he knew the answer to. He was not sure of the meaning of a marginal tax rate.

Having worked with the entire spectrum of incomes, I find that most people are not sure what their marginal tax rate is. In fact most people are not sure what is meant by the marginal tax rate. The easiest way to explain it is to review the tax tables below. You'll notice these are for individuals in the year of 2014. These are only for federal income taxes so you will need to check with your local accountant for your particular states tax rate.

Income Tax 2014		
Married Filing Jointly:	$0 - $18,150	$0 + 10%
$18,151	$73,800	$1,815 + 15%
$73,801	$148,850	$10,162.50 + 25%
$148,851	$226,850	$28,925 + 28%
$226,851	$405,100	$50,765 + 33%
$405,101	$457,600	$109,587.50 + 35%
$457,601	–	$127,962.50 + 39.6%
Single:	$0 - $9,075	$0 + 10%
$9,076	$36,900	$907.50 + 15%
$36,901	$89,350	$5,081.25 + 25%
$89,351	$186,350	$18,193.75 + 28%
$186,351	$405,100	$45,353.75 + 33%
$405,101	$406,750	$117,541.25 + 35%
$406,751	–	$118,118.75 + 39.6%

Capital Gains Tax		
Tax Bracket	1 year or less	Greater than 1 year
0% to 15%	Ordinary Income	0%
25% to 35%	Ordinary Income	15%
39.6%	Ordinary Income	20%

Sources: IRS, Rev. Proc 2013-35, 2014; IRS, Tax Topics - Topic 409 Capital
Gains and Losses, December 12, 2013; Social Security Administration,
Taxation of Social Security Benefits, as of January 8, 2014; Internal Revenue
Code. Title 26 Section 1411. Imposition of Tax. as of January 7. 2014; Social

Let's make sure we understand Ted's confusion concerning the average tax rate versus the marginal tax rate. First let's define average tax rate. It is calculated by dividing the total tax you have paid in a particular year by your gross income. Assume that Ted and Ruth paid $24,137 in federal income taxes and their income was $150,000 ($24,137/$150,000= 16%). So Ted and Ruth's <u>average</u> income tax rate was 16%.

The marginal tax rate is a little more difficult to calculate. It is the tax rate on the **last dollar of earnings**. Using the tax tables I gave you above go to the table entitled Joint Returns and Surviving Spouse. You'll notice there is no 16% tax bracket. The 16% tax Ted and Ruth are paying is the average tax of all of the brackets on the table. Keep in mind some deductions were taken from income where there was no tax paid. Let's assume Ted and Ruth take a standard deduction which is $12,400. In addition they have a personal and dependency exemption of $3,950 each. As you know that means they pay no income tax on those two amounts (i.e.,$20,300). The rest of their income is taxable income to which we apply the tax tables. The following example will make it clearer.

$150,000 Earned Income
($12,400 Standard Deduction)
$137,600
($ 7,900 Personal Exemption ($3950 x 2)
$129,700 Adjusted Gross Income
$ (18,150 of the taxable income is taxed at 10% =$1,815)
$ 111,550
$ (55,649 of the taxable income is taxed @ 15%=$8,347)
$ (55,901 the balance of income is taxed @ 25%=$13,975)

Total federal tax equals $ 24,137 which equals 16% of his income. This is the average tax. The marginal tax is the 25 % federal tax levied on the last half of his income. Knowing the marginal rate is important because every time Ted has additional income it will be taxed at this higher rate of 25%. If we assume Ted had an income of $225,000 a year then his marginal bracket could be as high as 33% federal. When we understand what the marginal tax bracket is we can see how important it might be to repositioning of assets. For instance if Ted and Ruth had $100,000 in a taxable Certificate of Deposit earning 4% interest (an average CD rate over the last 40 years) they would earn approximately $4000 over the course of a year. If his marginal tax rate is 28% then how much of that $4000 of additional income would go to the tax man and how much would be kept in Ted's account? If your answer is $1120 to the tax man, you are 100% correct. As financial planners, we feel good tax planning may be as important as good asset allocation. It doesn't seem wise to shop your CD to get half a percent higher rate of interest when you are ignoring the fact you may be giving up four or five times as much in potentially unnecessary income taxes.

So far we've only covered federal income taxes. Many of us live in states with a state income tax levied on earnings and investment returns. As a resident of Oklahoma our top income bracket is over 5%. For Ted and Ruth that brings their marginal bracket up to 30.25% (i.e., 25% federal and 5.25% state).

Saving income taxes is not an easy thing to do. I love my country and want to support it. At the same time I know the government does a very effective job of collecting taxes. One of the suggestions I make often is for clients to meet with their accountant during his off-season so they can ask about more effective ways to reduce their tax burden. Why during the off-season? How much time and benefit can your accountant provide if you bring your tax data to him on February10. If your accountant is like mine he is so busy he can hardly get his head out of the tax returns to say hello to you. Even if he comes up with tax suggestions how can you do anything about them since you are already two months into a new year? By meeting with him during his off-season he has time to focus on you and your situation while there is time to make adjustments.

If you're a business owner or a self-employed professional, I suggest you and your tax advisor meet three times during the year...perhaps in May, September and December. This way you have an opportunity to plan for the taxes and make adjustments during the year as you see how your income is developing. Don't expect your accountant to do this at no charge. During these sessions you are doing tax planning. Preparing a tax return is billed separately. The tax planning fee hopefully will save much more in tax savings.

Estate Taxes…"you mean I pay taxes all my life and then get taxed again at death?

As the meeting with Ted and Ruth progressed we completed our discussion of income taxes. Then I wrote in big and bold letters 'ESTATE TAXES'. Ted joked about the old adage that there are only two things for certain in life... death and taxes! Ted said, "I guess you're going to tell us now that everything we've acquired to this point is going to be taxed again when we die." Leaning back in my chair I thought about the correct answer to Ted's question. "Ted", I said, "the good news is that in the short run there will not be any death taxes (i.e., estate taxes) due on your assets. The bad news is that if you live a long life the amount of death taxes could devastate your estate." And then I showed them the chart below.

Estate Tax Exclusion		
2013	$5,250,000	40% tax rate
2014	$5,340,000	40% tax rate
Gift Tax Exclusion:	$14,000/year	$5,340,000/lifetime
Generation Skipping Tax:	–	$5,340,000/lifetime

Federal Estate Tax

In general, Federal estate taxes (i.e., death tax) are levied as property is passed from one generation to the next generation. Upon the death of a spouse property can pass to the surviving spouse with no death tax due; however, at the death of the surviving spouse there is a death tax levied (i.e., called a Federal Estate Tax). As few as 15 years ago the tax was levied on amounts passing to the next generation in excess of $1,000,000. The top tax rate was 55%. That is right, 55% of property exceeding $1,000,000 when to the tax collector. Currently the $1,000,000 exemption has been raised for the year 2014 to $5,340,000 per spouse. Therefore, a family can pass on a total of $10,680,000 (i.e., $5,340,000 per spouse) with no tax. Any amount over the $10,680,000 will bear a top tax bracket of 40%.

Ted and Ruth's estate will probably never reach these amounts so there was no discussion of this area. However, many people in this great country will face this very significant tax and should be aware of its consequence. If you are in that situation, work with your advisor to reduce this potential burden.

To the Rescue... some tax savings ideas

The estate tax is one tax, with proper planning, can be totally avoided as a burden to the family. This certainly is not an area for do-it-yourselfers. The estate tax laws are very complicated and the tax can be exceptionally high. My suggestion is threefold:

- First, look at your current situation to see if there is the potential for income or estate tax problems.
- Second, don't stop if there are not any current problems created by the size of your estate. Instead, make a projection of the value in 20 to 30 years (depending on your current age) to determine if a reasonable net increase in your estate would create a tax levy on your assets...
- Finally, team up with a good financial planner and estate planning attorney to develop a strategy so that your family, the people you love and the organizations you support such as church, schools, charities will receive the assets and not federal and state government.

I am not an accountant or an attorney; therefore, I cannot give tax or legal advice. There are a number of good methods of avoiding the tax burdens for those who have had a successful life of saving and investing.

Bypass Trusts

Most attorneys and financial planners suggest a good step in avoiding or minimizing taxes is to set up a 'bypass' trust. The bypass trust provision typically is added to a testamentary or revocable living trust. The goal is to assure both spouses get the full benefit of their federal estate tax exemption. Remember the estate tax exemption in 2014 is over $5 million per spouse.

I have seen a large number of the estates over my lifetime and most of them have not had the bypass trust provision. That doesn't mean their wills and trusts were poorly drawn, it just means at the time they did the estate planning they were not taking into consideration the potential growth of their assets. If their assets don't increase there is no need for the bypass provision and so the attorneys leave it off. Remember, the top tax rate on an estate is 40% in 2014 and beyond. By missing out on proper planning the estate could be paying an extra $400,000 in death taxes on every $1,000,000 over the exemption.

Another tax saving idea... Wealth Replacement Account

Below are two estate transfer ideas that we have used effectively in the past. See what you think of them. They may be of benefit to you and your family at some time.

The first idea some find attractive is the Wealth Replacement Account. It involves transferring capitol from one account into another account. The concept is quite simple yet very powerful. A real life case may be the best way to illustrate the concept. The case involves a lady who has been a widow for the last 10 years. She is in her mid sixties. We will call her Florence. Florence has three adult children and four grand children. She has recently remarried. Florence is concerned she will die without leaving any assets to her children or grandchildren. Currently she has income from Social Security and her deceased husband's pension and her investments.

She has more than enough income to meet all needs. From the excess monthly income she will transfer $400 per month into a cash value life insurance policy. The policy immediately provides $450,000 of death benefit payable to the three adult children. Instead of the $400 per month (that she is not spending) accumulating in her bank account it will accumulate in the cash value of her life insurance policy. Should she need the cash much of it will be available through a policy loan. God forbid, should she die in the first year of the contract, her children will receive over 90 times what would have accumulated in her bank saving account (i.e., $450,000 of death benefit vs $4,800 in the savings account). Florence is comfortable knowing the death benefit will be a legacy for her children even if she spends down her other assets.

47

The second idea is called the Wealth Replacement Trust. Currently the estate tax provides a $5,000,000 exemption to each spouse so the example below is not necessary and therefore does not apply. However, over the last 101 years the United State Congress has enacted estate taxes and done away with estate taxes four times. With our Government being so much in debt there is a good possibility the Federal Estate Taxes will be revised again with a much smaller exemption. Therefore, I feel you some day in the future may need to consider using this concept to protect your asset from the tax man.

We will use Ted and Ruth for this illustration since their estate used this exact planning not too many year ago. Let me explain how some brilliant people have developed this concept called the Wealth Replacement Trust. As the name implies, the purpose of the trust is to replace the wealth that is lost to the estate tax collector. Here's the idea in a nutshell. In our example above, Ted and Ruth's estate, several years ago under the previous estate tax rules, would owe $350,000 to the tax collector at Ruth's death. The only way to avoid this tax is to give the $700,000 that is taxable to a charity. Assuming this is not in their plans, the tax will have to be paid. Enter the wealth accumulation trust to save the day (or at least the kids' money). Here's the simplified version. The trust is drawn during Ted and Ruth's life time. They have no ownership in the trust... typically the children are the owners and the beneficiaries of the trust. The trust then applies for and purchases a special type of life insurance policy on the lives of Ted and Ruth. The policy amount is the estimated amount that will be paid in death taxes and perhaps attorney fees. Hence the name wealth replacement trust…the life insurance death benefits paid at the death of the survivor will reimburse the beneficiaries for the taxes that will have to be paid. The policy used most often is called a survivor joint life insurance policy. The trust becomes the owner and the beneficiary of the policy. The problem is the children typically don't have the money to pay for this life insurance so where do the funds come from? Remember our earlier calculation that the estate taxes would be $350,000. If this is the case the $350,000 really will not pass on to the children (i.e., sooner or later the government is going to get every single nickel of it in the form of an estate tax). So the brilliant guys who developed the wealth replacement trust understood this and decided some of the money that belong to mom and dad could be used upfront to pay for the life insurance in the wealth replacement trust. In effect the life insurance is not costing the family anything because the money wasn't going to be there for them anyway. It's like getting insurance for nothing but it's pretty close to it.

On a personal note, I remember in 1992 when my mother-in-law, Eva Tidball, died. She was a wonderful lady who was loved dearly by her four daughters and sons-in-law. Eva and her husband Paul, who died in 1987, raised their four daughters on a wheat farm in western Oklahoma. Starting out with nothing they scraped, scratched and eked out an existence during those early years on the farm. My wife was 12 before they had a bathroom in the house. Farming was tough and second jobs were a must to survive. Somehow they not only survived but prospered.

As I said Paul died first and Eva followed a few years later. I remember the sad day when the four girls gathered in their parent's home. By now the estate had been settled and the death tax payment was due. No federal tax was due, but the state levied $28,000 in death taxes. As the four girls sat around the table they cried as they each wrote out a check for $7,000 payable to The State of Oklahoma. Believe me, folks, my wife and her sisters weren't crying because of the money, they were crying because their mom and dad had worked so hard on that farm for so many years that it just didn't seem right that the government would take part of what they had accumulated. The experience taught me paying of these taxes is not only a logical, and economic issue, but one that deals with the heart.

Summary...

- Be aware of the high cost of both income and estate taxes.
- Realize careful planning can help lessen both.
- Realize these are complicated areas and you may need help from estate planning attorneys, CPAs and financial planners.

Chapter 5
Eight Categories of Insurance

Boring! That's my feeling about insurance and risk management issues. Policies seem to be written by Philadelphia lawyers so that no one can want to read them or understand them. Besides, if you try to read them, they put you to sleep in three minutes. Nevertheless, risk management/insurance plays a vital role in financial security. You can accumulate a fortune over your lifetime and lose it all in a split second, by an unwise lane change on the highway.

We live in a litigious society and unfortunately juries many times go along with outrageously large settlements. Do you remember the McDonald's hot coffee spill a number of years ago? Wasn't that claim settled for $1.7 million? Another example, involved the famous golfer Sam Snead. Over his lifetime he won 85 tournaments. After retiring to Florida he was involved in an auto accident and the judgment against him was **more than he had won in all of those 85 tournaments**. We have to realize you and I certainly are not insulated from these events. We need to be prudent and protect ourselves. Keeping in mind this is not the most exciting topic, I will be brief yet thorough.

Let's visit with Ted and Ruth again in their next meeting. Spring is trying to break the back of Old Man Winter and the Dunleavy's have arrived on a beautiful sunny day with the temperature close to 60°. At this meeting Ruth and Ted brought pictures of their cruise in the Caribbean. I remark, "You both seem to have adjusted nicely to retirement. Isn't this the second extended trip you've taken since retiring?" We spent a few minutes talking about this first year and a half away from his job. I began our meeting with, "When we started this financial journey our objective was to get your financial house in order. So far we have developed a livable and believable retirement plan as well as discussing your income and estate taxes. The next step in your 'road map to getting your financial house in order is risk management and insurance'. Tell me about the method you follow for reviewing your various insurance products."

Ted, the engineer, likes working with numbers and he responds, "I feel our insurance program is pretty sound. We have worked with the same agent for a number of years and feel comfortable and secure with his advice. He has placed us with a national company we feel is financially strong and able to pay claims. Nowadays we don't do much except pay the premiums. Is that what you mean?"

I replied, "It gives me a good idea of what you're doing. When was the last time you had your policies audited? What about the last time you had your agent shop with various companies to see if your rates could be reduced? You probably know the answer to these questions as well as I do. Most likely it has been 10 to 15 years since there was an overall audit done of all the policies and perhaps as long since the contracts were actually shopped for better benefits or lower rates."

Insurance Audit

We typically think of an audit being done by accountants to check the accuracy of a company's books. An audit for insurance purposes is designed to check for gaps in coverage and policy provisions and definitions. Keep in mind that policy audits should be done on all the forms of insurance you own. This includes life insurance, property and casualty insurance, health insurance, disability income insurance, and umbrella liability insurance. If you have several agents who handle different types of insurance for you, you will need to contact each of those agents to do an audit over the coverage they provide. At the time of the audit you might also check on the premium payments to make sure they are currently competitive in the marketplace. At times we have seen clients reduce their premium rates from $200 per year all the way to $2,100 per year. In the next section we will review each area of insurance you might own and discuss some of the things to look for concerning those policies.

1. Auto and home insurance (i.e., called property and casualty)

What can I tell you about auto and homeowners insurance you don't already know? This is pretty basic stuff, isn't it? There are just a few things I want to make sure you take into consideration. First call your agent (or better yet, call a competing agent) and ask for a repricing. Over the last several years, some automobile and homeowners insurance companies have dropped the policy premiums. If you just continue renewing the premium without doing any comparison shopping, it's unlikely your agent will volunteer to re-shop for you. Most likely he is too busy to volunteer. In addition his sales commissions will drop if the premium goes down. Not a lot of incentive on their part, is there? The second thing I suggest is to have your agent or another agent review all of your property and casualty policies for gaps in the coverage or limits which are too low. After all, the values of your property may have increased substantially over the years and the coverage may not have increased. Perhaps there is a gap in coverage should a claim occur.

Here is a personal example which cost me money. As your coach, I'm a little embarrassed to mention my not following my own rules. When my kids were all still at home we had five old cars and we were paying insurance premiums on all five. One of the cars we had bought when it was almost new and had it fully insured. Seven years later, that same car had very little value yet we had continued the same insurance coverage with the same premium as I paid the first year. When we realized my mistake we dropped the comprehensive coverage (i.e., the car had almost no insurable value). We just kept the liability coverage. That mistake cost me several hundred dollars a year for a number of years.

While you are checking on your policies provisions, please check to be sure your policy is a replacement value policy. The benefit is substantial. Should there be a claim, for instance on your home, a policy pays to have the structure replaced at current costs. The replacement value provision may cost a little more but in my estimation it is well worth it. This feature is very important when it comes time to collecting on a policy claim. As the agent is checking on the policy limits and the premiums, have him give you some comparison prices for different deductibles. The higher the deductible is the lower the premium will be.

As your savings and investments have grown you should be in a better position to self-insure yourself for the smaller claims. For instance, when Ted and Ruth were first married, they had a lot of expenses and not much income or savings. Low deductibles may have fit them very well. Now their savings have grown substantially, it is probably more economical for them to have a $500 or $1,000 or higher deductible. The theory being if there is no claim for three or four years the premium savings will more than offset the higher deductible amount.

2. Umbrella liability coverage

Before finishing the discussion regarding their property and casualty insurance I asked one final question, "Do you have an umbrella liability policy?" Ruth replied, "Tell me what you mean by an umbrella liability policy. I don't think we have one". I explained an umbrella liability policy provides liability coverage over and above the liability you have on your homeowners or auto insurance. Umbrella policies range in benefits up to $1,000,000, $2,000,000 and more. As an example, if your current automobile coverage is $250,000/500,000, and you are in an automobile accident which is your fault, if the judge were to award the person in the other car $800,000, your policy would pay $250,000. The balance would have to be paid from your personal assets. With a million-dollar umbrella liability policy, the umbrella policy would pay the excess claim over the $250,000 up to the million dollar limit. Umbrella liability policies are very inexpensive (i.e., a $1,000,000 liability limit may cost less than $200 per year) and very beneficial.

3. Disability income insurance

This type of insurance pays in the event the insured is disabled and cannot work. For Ted and Ruth, there really is no need because Ted is at the point of retirement. However, if we were talking to their children, disability income insurance is critical. Many families are only a few paychecks away from bankruptcy. Without a paycheck how does the mortgage get paid or groceries purchased? Please understand I'm not talking about having the flu for two weeks. I'm speaking of a long-term disability lasting six months or longer. These events can bankrupt a family.

Disability income insurance may be purchased through the employer, an association the insured is a member, or individually. My recommendation is to first purchase as much as possible through your employer. Typically the premiums are reasonable and it is conveniently deducted automatically from your paycheck. If a group plan thru an association or your employer is not available or in the event there is a low limit on the amount of disability income through the employer, then individual coverage is your only options. .

Disability income policies have three variables:

- The waiting period
- The monthly benefit amount
- The length of payments

The Waiting Period: The insured must be disabled for a certain number of days before the insurance company begins paying the claim. The waiting periods typically are 30 days, 60 days, 90 days, 180 days, and 365 days. The longer the waiting period the lower the premium will be.

The Monthly Benefit Amount: This is the monthly amount received by the insured should they become disabled. Normally the amounts are limited to 60% to 70% of the person's pre-disability income. As you might imagine, the higher the benefit amount, the higher the premium will be.

Length of payments: This refers to how long the insurance policy will pay in the event the insured is disabled. Benefit periods typically are two years, five years, and to age 65. The longer the benefit period is the higher the premium will be. Although the length of payments on a plan which pays benefits to age 65 may be 20 times larger than a 2 year benefit plan. The premiums on the benefit to 65 is usually is no more than twice the premium for the two year benefit plan. Personally I feel the plan that will pay benefits to age 65 is by far the most beneficial option.

4. Health insurance

What can we say about health insurance? Three words sum it up... it is expensive! Once the employee reaches age 65, they are eligible for Medicare. The problem I see too often is the employee and or the employee's spouse retire before they are eligible for Medicare. If fortunate their employer has a health care plan which will extend until they are eligible for Medicare benefits.

I own a small financial planning company that provides group health insurance for all our employees. When my wife and I were in the 60 age range, the group insurance premium paid for my wife and I was over $1000 per month each ($24,200 per year)...**Ouch**! If Ted's wife is age 62 when he retires at 65 she will not be eligible for Medicare benefits for three more years. They now have only two options because his company does not provide for medical insurance for Ruth after he retires. The options are:

1) Buy individual health insurance for Ruth. There are two obstacles to individual health insurance. The first one of course is the cost. It is costly to buy health insurance on Ruth at her age of 62; however, I think this is the lesser of the two problems. In my opinion the biggest problem is insurability. Insurance companies always investigate health and pre-existing conditions to qualify you as a risk for a health insurance policy. How the heck can you reach age 62 and not have some pre-existing conditions? It "ain't" going to happen! There are two solutions to this problem.

First, she is eligible for COBRA which will provide coverage for 18 months. COBRA is the guarantee option to continue on the employer health plan for 18 months without having to answer health questions. A problem arises, at Ruth's age, COBRA will run out 18 months before she reaches Medicare eligibility. Also the employee is required to pay the full premium on Cobra (both the normal employee cost and the employer cost).

Second, the availability of Obama Care provides another option. With Obama Care, a wonderful option is available for the people who are in the position of being without coverage and having a 'preexisting medical condition'. Termination of employment qualifies Ruth for a condition called a "major life event". Because of the 'major life event'(i.e., termination of employment) Ruth can qualify to enroll in an Obama Care policy with no pre existing conditions.

2) Have no health insurance and hope she does not have a major claim. In my opinion going without health coverage is taking a serious risk. I have had a few experiences with medical claims. One of the financial planners in my office had a mild heart attack several years ago. She was in the hospital just overnight after doctors put in three stints to the arteries surrounding her heart. Her bill was $44,000. This was with no open-heart surgery. What if it was a stroke and you were in intensive care for 10 days?

Personally, I went to the emergency room in July of 2007 after I became lightheaded during a workout with my trainer, Larry Krutka (if you live in Tulsa he is the best). The hospital ran the normal tests to make certain I was okay (thank goodness I was). Guess what the bill was for three hours in the emergency room? The bill was just under $5,000. I'm not trying to scare anybody into buying health insurance. I don't sell health insurance. I just know medical problems can devastate financial plans. In my opinion a family may need to postpone retiring before Medicare eligibility if a good solution cannot be found to the health insurance issue.

5. Medicare

Once a person is 65 years of age, they are eligible for Medicare and a Medicare Supplement. These are two separate items and must be applied for individually. Even if a person is continuing to work and is covered under their company group health insurance policy, it is important to notify the benefits department. The best source of information on Medicare is the Government web site Medicare.Gov. You may also call their 1 800 772 1213

6. Medicare Supplement

When Ted turns age 65 he may apply for a Medicare supplement policy. Medicare is designed to pay many of the costs but not 100% of everything. The Medicare supplement policy is designed to fill in gaps not covered by Medicare. Hence some call this coverage Medi Gap coverage. Medicare supplements come in a number of different varieties based on how much of the Medicare expenses will be covered. Ted and Ruth have the option of choosing a supplement policy which range from Plan A to Plan F. Some plans have lower premiums and pay fewer of the expenses not covered by Medicare. The most expensive plan is Plan F. This plan pays 100% of the items not covered by Medicare. As you might expect it has the highest premium.

A number of different companies sell Medicare supplements. It is important for you to know each policy, although sold by different companies, has been designed by the Federal Government. Each policy has exactly the same benefits and same benefit payouts. However, various companies selling these policies are allowed to charge differently. This is a requirement of the federal government and is a benefit to you. In this way it is easier to compare various company premiums for the Medicare supplement you decide to purchase. The only difference between the contracts is the premium the insurance company charges for a particular plan. In other words, all Plan 'A's have exactly the same contractual features and pay out benefits.

When Ted turns age 65 (as well as anyone turning age 65), it is important for him to make an application for the Medicare supplement within six months. This is what we might call a free look. During the six months after turning 65 you can apply for a Medicare supplement policy and have no pre-existing conditions placed on the contract. That holds true if you have just been diagnosed with cancer or had a major heart attack. Once you have passed the six months free look you run the risk of having a rider placed on a contract that could limit the coverage paid on certain pre-existing claims.

7. Long-term care insurance

As Ted, Ruth and I sat around the table discussing the various forms of insurance, Ted said "Skip, Ruth and I have talked a lot about Long-Term Care Insurance. We understand some people feel it is very valuable. In our case we have decided against it due to the expense plus we feel our assets are sufficient to pay any of those expenses should they come up. Besides we're both in good health and we take good care of ourselves."

As a financial planner I have struggled with Ted's reasoning. Understand every situation is unique and has to be examined individually. I do have a general philosophy concerning long-term care. In working with hundreds of retirees, I've come to the conclusion there two groups of people who do not need long-term care. The first group is those with very modest income and assets. The second group is the very wealthy. I know those are vague terms so let me wrap some details around them to help you understand my thoughts.

The first group of modest income and assets do not need long-term care because should one of the spouses need home health care or nursing home care they will fairly rapidly spend down their assets and be eligible for Medicaid. Medicaid, for those not familiar with it, is a governmental program to pay long-term care expenses once a person's assets have been reduced to approximately $2000.

I don't have a hard and fast rule about the definition of modest assets. Perhaps it is less than $70,000. Much of the assets might be tied up in a house and automobile so only $10,000 to $15,000 in cash or equities may be available. You can imagine those funds will go quickly leaving a person eligible for Medicaid. Since long-term care insurance is somewhat pricey, it makes sense not to take this type of person's limited income to pay for something the government is going to provide anyway.

On the other hand I don't believe those with significant income and wealth need long-term care insurance. They can probably very easily afford the additional outlay of home health care or a nursing home without risking bankruptcy. Some of my colleagues argue people should purchase long-term care since they have significant income for the premium. The benefit my colleagues argue is there will be more of the estate left for the children or for gifts to nonprofit organizations or charities. A point well taken, but my thought is there will still be a considerable amount available for children and those nonprofits, even if they don't have long term care insurance.

Like other forms of insurance a long-term care policy requires an application with medical history to be completed. In the earlier health section we discussed pre-existing conditions. Any pre-existing conditions can certainly affect a person being qualified to purchase long-term care insurance. As you can imagine insurance companies do not want to insure people who they feel are a bad medical risk.

When purchasing long-term care you have three variables to consider:

- Waiting Periods
- Benefit amounts
- Length of Benefits

Waiting Period: The waiting period refers to the length of time a person must wait before a claim is paid by the insurance company (i.e. similar to a deductible). Benefit periods are 30 days, 60 days, 100 days, 180 days, and 365 days. As you might imagine, the longer the waiting period the lower the insurance premium will be.

Benefit Amount: The benefit amount is the payment, on a monthly basis to be received once the client is eligible to receive payment.

Normally the benefit amount varies from $50 per day to as high as $250 per day. In order to determine the proper amount of coverage an individual needs to take into consideration the cost for home health care and/or nursing home care in the area they reside. In northeast Oklahoma the best source of this information is a nonprofit organization named Life Senior Services. Life Senior Services has three offices in this area which servicing senior citizens. Similar organizations are located throughout the United States. They are the best sources information regarding expenses and facilities. They provide a wonderful service to the senior community.

My personal experience is these facilities (assisted living centers or nursing homes) are much more expensive than most people realize. In the mid-90s, when my mother went into an assisted living center, the cost was over $1900 per month. My mom's income was approximately $1150 a month. It doesn't take a Philadelphia lawyer to understand this is deficit spending. She eventually moved into a full care nursing center with a cost of $3,000 per month. When you have an experience like this it is easy to understand how people deplete their assets and be become eligible for Medicaid. Eating up all of a family's assets to pay for home health care or nursing home care is sometimes referred to as the 'Medicaid spend down'.

Length of benefit

The length of benefit refers to the length of time the policy will pay benefits after a claim has been made. Policies typically pay benefits for two years, three years, four years, five years, and lifetime (most lifetime policies are not written today). The longer the benefits are paid, the higher the premium will be. It's difficult to decide the length of benefit because no one knows exactly how long benefits may be needed. There are a number of the factors I take into consideration when recommending long-term care insurance coverage. According to a national study, the average stay in a nursing home is 2 1/2 years. Taking this fact into consideration as well as the assets and income of the family helps to determine the length of benefit to purchase. Personally my wife and I have a benefit plan of five years. Hopefully all the money we spend on our long-term care will be totally wasted and we will never have to collect on it. However, if we do need to collect on it for five years we will have received in benefits many times over what we paid in premiums.

In an article entitled "A Federal Case for Long-Term Care" by Employee Benefit News (October 2010) the officer estimated roughly half of those aged 65 today will be admitted to a nursing home at some point in their lives. The author also concluded the average cost of nursing home care in the United States is $70,000. Fortunately in Oklahoma the expenses are less. Regardless, these are numbers that none of us, in my opinion, can disregard.

Source: Genworth Financial, 2007 Cost of Care Survey, March 2007, pp. 26-27

8. Life insurance

By this point in our meeting we were all getting a little tired. Ted had already had two cups of coffee and slipped out to the bathroom once. You know how it is us with us guys as we get a little older...the bathroom breaks are more frequent. I looked across the table at Ruth and ask her specifically, "How do you feel about the amount of life insurance you have on Ted's life?" Ruth thought for a moment then answered, "Now that the children are grown and we have almost no debt, there doesn't seem to be much need for insurance. Thanks to the retirement planning you helped us do last year I know the assets Ted and I have accumulated will be sufficient to take care of me for as long as I live if, God forbid, Ted were to die."

Didn't Ruth sum it up nicely? An enviable position most retirees should be in when it comes to their life insurance needs. Ideally, in my opinion, my clients shouldn't need life insurance when they get to retirement age. There are always a few exceptions, but it should be the general goal. If there is no more need for life insurance then the premiums paid for life insurance can be saved, leaving more money for the family's budget during the retirement years.

The three exceptions I see are:

1. Families who have substantial debt
2. Families with additional responsibilities
3. Families planning for the estate taxes which become due at their deaths.

As with all other forms of insurance I suggest the policies, if they are still in force, be audited and checked for competitiveness every three to five years. There have been numerous improvements and cost reductions in the life insurance industry over the last 30 years. Therefore a careful review and comparison of current policies should be made. My basic position is the best option is to keep the policies you currently own. If you are comparing a policy you currently have in force, any new policy you are considering should be substantially better for you to replace the current policy. If you do decide to replace a policy make sure you document carefully all the facts the agent is giving you. Make certain you are comparing apples with apples and the illustrations are based on reliable factors. I am a trusting person but I am also aware of the fact an agent presenting a new policy has a vested interest in your buying from him (i.e., the commission). Be very careful to document and verify all of the information in your comparison. President Reagan put it best, "Trust but verify".

In the back of this section there is a form letter we suggest be mailed to all life insurance companies, including your employer benefit department, to verify current beneficiaries. Don't take for granted the beneficiaries are set up properly. We all are very busy and sometimes things we intend to do don't get done. I cannot tell you how many times I have found beneficiaries to be incorrect, even after the insured swore it was correct.

About 12 years ago I gave a speech at a support group for widows and widowers. As the meeting was coming to an end, a lady in her late forties approached me. She said, "Skip, may I tell you my story? My husband has been dead a little over six months. This was his second marriage. We had been married five years before his death. When I filed the insurance claim with his employer I was shocked to find his first wife was still named as the beneficiary. The policy was for $50,000. Contractually, there was nothing I could do to receive the policy proceeds. His hospital stay and funeral cost have left me with $25,000 of debt. I miss him so and yet I am so angry about the bind it has put me in."

Do you see why we don't take people at their word when they tell us their beneficiaries are properly set up? I would also check named beneficiaries on your IRAs and your 401(k). There was recently an article in the paper concerning a teacher in the New York City school system who died. She had been employed for over 35 years and had a retirement account of over $800,000. Guess who the beneficiary was? Not like our widow above. The primary beneficiary on her retirement account was her mother and the contingent beneficiary was her sister. This deceased teacher had been married for over 28 years, but had never changed the beneficiary. A simple oversight...yes, but a $800,000 costly oversight!

Earlier, the suggestion was made to audit and cost compare your insurance policies every few years. There are several reasons that old policies may not be as competitive as they once were. These are some of those reasons:

1. Mortality Charges... mortality charges are the assumptions of how many people of a certain group will die over a period of time. People are living longer. In 1965 when I came into the financial services business, life insurance companies were using the 1960 Commissioners Standard Ordinary Mortality Table. This table has been consistently updated and now the 2000 Commissioners Standard Ordinary Mortality Table is used. Insurance costs have decreased substantially as people live longer. Your policy premiums may be based on an out of date mortality table causing you to pay higher premiums.

2. Company Expenses... when I first entered the financial services field home office employees were using large desk calculators, manual typewriters, and mimeograph machines. Now we have incredibly fast computers, word processing programs, fax machines, e-mail, etc., allowing companies to do more business faster and with fewer employees. This has helped lowered the cost of insurance.

3. Asset Management... because of the above technological changes and more savvy and experienced investment departments, insurance companies may get better returns on their assets.

These above three factors have all worked in favor of the insured. Competition has caused rates to decline so don't just assume your policy is still competitive.

Chapter 6
Tools to Protect and Grow Wealth

As Ted and Ruth enter the retirement phase of their life, we might assume they would be comfortable and adequately prepared for investment decisions they face. After all, Ted is an engineer and has been saving or investing money for most of his working life. Shouldn't 40 years experience prepare you adequately? How does Ted feel about his future investment decisions?

Ted said, "Skip, I need help. Truthfully, I am still confused about where my money should be invested so that Ruth and I never run out of income. When I was in the accumulating years of my life, I did not worry when my 401k account declined as the stock market fell. I felt I could ride out a beaten down stock market. I'm in a new ballgame now. Market declines worry me since we are taking withdrawals each month." Ruth chimed in, "I also worry. Most of my lady friends and I agree we need to put all of our money in something without risk."

Ted and Ruth have hit upon an area where retirees struggle. What is the best investment philosophy to adopt at retirement? In the last fifteen years we have had two major stock market declines (i.e., 2000 2001 in 2002 and late 2007 through early 2009). These declines weigh heavily on our minds as Ted and Ruth struggle with the burden of creating reliable sources of income they won't outlive. Financing retirement seems more uncertain and complex.

Let's discuss this change in financial mindset as Ted and Ruth transition from full-time work into retirement. It sounds easy, it has lulled many people during years preceding retirement into a complacency. The core principles for building a lifetime of wealth through financial assets are quite straightforward. Consider investing early in life, keep investing regularly; build a well diversified portfolio strongly directed to equities in the early years. Then add an increasing share of less volatile fixed income assets as retirement age approaches. Haven't you heard your buddies discussing this basic strategy around the coffee pot? This basic strategy of 'age appropriate asset allocation' is based on the past performance of stocks, bonds, and short-term investments. It aims to avoid excessive caution early in life and excessive risk-taking in retirement. It enables an individual to use time to overcome adverse short-term moves in the equity market and thereby capture the long-term growth potential of stocks.

Equities, as a class, have significantly outperformed bonds for generations. Painful recent experience shows, stock markets can also decline rapidly and substantially. They may also deliver low returns for several years at a time. It is encouraging to note over longer time periods equities have historically more than made up for those periods of decline ((Source: The Art of Investing and Portfolio Management, page 44).

Historical Returns of Major Asset Classes.

Asset Class	Annualized Return, 1926 - 2006
U.S small-cap stocks	12.69%
U.S. large-cap stocks	10.39%
International stocks	11.57% *
Long-term government bonds	5.42%
Intermediate-term government bonds	5.28%
Treasury bills (cash)	3.71%

*1970-2006

Source: Ibbotson Associates

Age appropriate asset allocation strategies are designed to optimize a person's chances of benefiting from those long-term patterns. In the retirement savings arena, these strategies aim for accumulating wealth by a date individuals generally do have significant control over...their chosen time of retirement. America's financial services industry has done a fairly good job of educating the public about this 'accumulation' phase of lifetime financial management. I'm speaking of the 'accumulation phase' versus the 'distribution or withdrawal phase'. Millions of Americans broadly follow these principles in their 401(k) s and their IRA savings plans.

But at the point of transiting from accumulating assets to drawing on their life savings to provide retirement income, the situation becomes more complex. The stakes of making wise choices becomes more important. Retirees move from a situation in which they could count on long-term averages to correct short term declines in the market into a less forgiving world in which they must live with the reality of withdrawing from their account when it is down.

Let's look back in on Ted and Ruth. As I sit across the table from them I am rather sober in my comment, "Ted and Ruth, I think you'll agree with me when I say the financial services industry has not done a very good job of preparing their customers for this "distribution" phase of their financial lives. In 2003 a study by LIMRA International, Inc., a life insurance marketing research organization, found only one in five retirees or pre-retirees had a formal written plan for managing income, assets, and expenses during retirement. Many who do have "plans" base them on incorrect assumptions. Most retirees are simply "playing it by ear" – – a serious risk to their long-term financial health. The plans for 'accumulation' of wealth before retirement differ from the plans for 'distribution' during your retirement years. As we review your asset allocation model let's take into consideration these important risk factors which may affect all of your future decisions concerning your portfolio. These factors are: inflation risk, longevity risk, allocation risk, and excess withdrawals."

Ruth looked at me a little puzzled and said, "I don't understand how you avoid or eliminate these risk factors."

Chapter 7
Asset Allocation

This chapter will focus on answering Ruth's question. We will discuss some tools and studies developed in the financial services industry to better prepare retirees for making solid asset allocation decisions.

Perhaps the first and foundational decision to deal with is a retiree's asset allocation. As financial planners, we talk of these as risk tolerance profiles. The profiles determine the level of risk (or volatility) a person will accept in their investment allocation. Below are six common profiles:

- **Profile One: Capital Preservation.** This profile has approximately 20% in a diversified portfolio of US equities and 80% in fixed income/bonds/cash

- **Profile Two: Balanced Income.** This profile has approximately 30% in a diversified portfolio of United States equities, 10% international equities, 60% fixed income/bonds/cash.

- **Profile Three: Balanced.** This profile has approximately 40% in a diversified portfolio of United States equities, 20% international equities, and 40% fixed income/bonds/cash.

- **Profile Four: Balanced Growth.** This profile has approximately 50% in a diversified portfolio of United States equities, 25% international equities, 25% fixed income/bonds/cash.

- **Profile Five: Growth.** This profile has approximately 60% in a diversified portfolio of United States equities, 30% international equities, 10% fixed income/bonds/cash

- **Profile Six: Aggressive growth.** This profile has approximately 60% in a diversified portfolio of United States equities and 40% in a diversified portfolio of international equities.

After completing the risk tolerance questionnaire and having an in-depth discussion about risk, it is determine Ted and Ruth are a Profile Three. You can look at the chart above and determine it to be a 'Balanced Portfolio', but in real life everyday terms what does that mean? There is no easy answer of exactly what any of these profiles might do in a particular period of time; however, you can get an idea of how various investment profiles may perform from studies of historical returns in the following pages.

Asset allocation is not an investment decision to take lightly or approach in a haphazard fashion. It requires a great deal of time and attention to do it correctly. Asset allocation is a critical part of your success as an investor. Reading the evening newspaper to see what stock prices have done today is not adequate. There are sophisticated skills involved in asset allocation... choosing asset classes; making assumptions about their future performance, risk correlation; and developing appropriate constraints all require skill and discipline. Without applying these skills to the process you may not achieve the full benefits of an efficient portfolio. The balance of the chapter will address what is required to develop an effective and efficient portfolio.

Many investors enlist financial advisors for assistance with asset allocation. However, care should be taken when enlisting the aid of an adviser. Some advisers focus more on selling products to their clients than on helping them allocate their assets in a way to deliver maximum benefits. Some advisors mean well but do not have the proper training and skill required for building an effective and efficient portfolio. It is important to assess your financial advisors asset allocation skills carefully. In a later chapter I will discuss the selection of a financial adviser.

As Ted and I reviewed his Profile 3 allocation he asked, "How to I know what a good asset mix is in each category?" I answered, "Ted, you asked an excellent question and one often answered incorrectly by investors. According to a landmark study of large pension funds *(Source: Financial Analyst Journal, May-June 1991)* asset allocation has been well documented as being the most important factor in portfolio performance. These experts studied the returns of 91 large pension funds from 1974 through 1983 to measure scientifically which factors were most important in determining investment performance.

The results of their research fundamentally reshaped how professional investors manage money. Too often individuals think market timing or specific securities selected are the most dominant and important factors in their portfolios performance.

In reality the way in which your assets are allocated among stocks, bonds, and cash and how they are rebalanced over time ultimately drives your portfolio returns. This study showed 90% of the portfolios variants is determined by how the assets are allocated; therefore, allocation is one of the most important decisions an investor can make. The study revealed only 4.6% of the portfolios variants was due to securities selection (i.e., picking the hottest mutual fund or stock). 1.8% of the portfolio variance was due to market timing (i.e., being in the market or out of the market at the right time). Yet market timing and security selection are what most people focus on. Source: Financial Analyst Journal, May-June 1991

Let me illustrate how powerful asset allocation is. Let us consider a hypothetical investor who bought a portfolio of a dozen large, technology stocks in 1997. Over the next three years there are enormous gains. The gains were not because the investor was a world-class stock whiz, but because large cap tech stocks were increasing at an unprecedented rate. Carrying this case further the portfolio would have come crashing down during the following three years. The investor would have been on a very unpleasant roller coaster ride. The volatile ride would have little to do with the individual stocks the investor held. Instead, the investor's asset allocation – – the decision to invest entirely in one asset class – – would be responsible for the variability of the performance.

If you want to maximize the probability of achieving your goals, the lesson is clear: first we determine the risk tolerance, the time horizon, and the long-term objectives. Once we've determined these then most of our time will be spent on making smart asset allocation decisions. Your goal should be to use advanced allocation strategies – – the kind used by investment companies' top minds – – when designing and maintaining your own investment portfolio.

Advanced Asset Allocation: A Nobel Prize Winning Approach

Most of us have heard the often cited cliché, "Don't put all your eggs in one basket". In the Bible (Ecclesiastes), God puts it this way, "divide your portion between seven, no eight, for no one knows what evil may befall the world". In my opinion advanced asset allocation applies this principle in a sophisticated, scientific manner. It uses proven mathematical formulas to determine which asset classes are most appropriate for an individual to own (based on their risk tolerance) as well as the optimal method of combining those asset classes to give the maximum diversification benefits. Essentially, advanced asset allocation answers two critical questions every investor should ask: Which asset class should I choose and how much of each asset class should I hold? Advanced asset allocation was first developed in 1952 by Harry Markowitz. He was a graduate student at the University of Chicago. Eventually his investment research became known as <u>Modern Portfolio Theory</u> and won Markowitz and several others, who pioneered Modern Portfolio Theory, the Nobel Prize in Economics in 1990.

Markowitz believed that investors are, by nature risk adverse. If the investment alternatives both provide the same potential return the typical investor will select the asset with the lowest risk. His research showed that investors expect to be compensated with higher returns if they are to take a higher risk. Therefore he set out with the idea of blending asset classes in a way to minimize risk, while also enhancing returns. His research revealed for every level of investment risk, there is a combination of assets which can generate the highest possible rate of return. The research focused on how various asset classes could be mixed to deliver the trade-off between risk and return. The research showed the risk of a particular stock was not the critical factor. What mattered more was the security's contribution to the overall risk of an <u>entire</u> portfolio. As you can imagine this was a new revelation.

Investment professionals began shifting their focus from analyzing the characteristics of individual securities toward examining the makeup of the entire portfolio and how it could be managed in terms of reward and risk.

74

Over the last thirty years, Modern Portfolio Theory has been universally accepted by a majority of professional investors. Modern Portfolio Theory is used by large investment firms, insurance companies, and pension firms as a guide to manage their entire investment portfolio. I was first exposed to modern portfolio theory in 1987 while attending a money-management seminar at the University of Ohio. This is a process the professionals can use as well as individuals in managing portfolios more effectively.

My goal is not to make you an expert in Modern Portfolio Theory. At the same time I want you to have exposure to all of the factors so you understand the basics of the process. Some of you may decide to apply modern portfolio theory on your own, while others will be hiring and investment professional. Should you hire a professional? Understanding the basics can also help to evaluate whether your professional is using some of the advanced asset allocation procedures.

To use Modern Portfolio Theory and advanced asset allocation strategies effectively, you need to understand a few important characteristics of the various asset classes. There are three characteristics: historical returns, historical risk, and correlation coefficients. We will call these the essential building blocks of advanced asset allocation. Over the next few pages I will explain these very briefly.

Advanced Asset Allocation... Essential building blocks for portfolio construction

Building Block Number 1.

The big picture—growth of $1 from 1925 to March 2007.

MARKET INVESTMENT RETURNS
Growth of $1 invested from January 1926 to March 2007

Source: Wilshire Associates

The above exhibit shows the long-term historical returns of the four major domestic asset classes. The returns run from the end of 1925 through mid-2007. The four classes are: small-cap stocks, large-cap stocks, bonds, and treasury bills (cash). There is a stark difference in the returns of some of these asset classes. We all agree stocks have offered the greatest potential return over time; however, many people might not realize one dollar invested in 1925 in a 30 day treasury bill would have a 2007 value of $19. That same dollar invested in large-company stocks in 1925 would have a value in 2007 of $2659.

Outside of the United States, we see that international equities also have delivered strong returns which have handily outpaced fixed income and cash investments over time. Foreign shares have averaged a gain of 10.1% annually from 1970 through 2007 (the longest length of time of data available for this asset class).

Keep in mind all of these returns are long-term averages. You cannot expect any individual year to match perfectly with these historical performances.

Building Block Number 2
Risk of Asset Classes

Historical risk of major asset classes

Asset class (Least Volatile to Most Volatile)	Standard Deviation	Annualized Long-Term Return
Treasury bills (cash)	0.88%	3.71%
Long-term government bonds	7.88%	5.42%
International stocks	16.45%	11.57%
S&P 500	19.16%	10.39%
U.S. small-cap stocks	29.28%	12.69%

Source: S&P

Investing would be easy if all we had to do was look at historical rates of return and there were no other factors to consider. We would pick the category which showed the highest rate of return and put all of our money there. What about risk/volatility? Higher potential returns go hand in hand with higher volatility. It is because of the risk/volatility, which goes along with stocks, enabling the investor to earn higher rate of returns over time in those equity investments. While equities have performed well historically over an extended time, but in the short run they can swing up and down wildly.

S&P 50 Index Year-by-Year Total Returns from 1926 - 2006
(All values shown in percentages)

<-20%	20%<x<-12%	-12%<x<-8%	-8%<x<0	0<x<8%	8%<x<12%	12%<x<20%	>20%
1930 -24.90	1973 -14.69	1929 -8.42	1934 -1.44	1947 5.71	1926 11.62	1944 19.75	1927 37.49
1931 -43.34		1932 -8.19	1939 -0.41	1948 5.50	1959 11.96	1949 18.79	1928 43.61
1937 -35.03		1940 -9.78	1953 -0.99	1956 6.56	1968 11.06	1952 18.37	1933 53.99
1974 -26.47		1941 -11.59	1977 -7.16	1960 0.47	1993 10.08	1964 16.48	1935 47.67
2002 -22.10		1946 -8.07	1981 -4.92	1970 4.01	2004 10.88	1965 12.45	1936 33.92
		1957 -10.78	1990 -3.10	1978 6.57		1971 14.30	1938 31.12
		1962 -8.73		1984 6.27		1972 18.99	1942 20.34
		1966 -10.06		1987 5.25		1979 18.61	1943 25.90
		1969 -8.50		1992 7.62		1986 18.67	1945 36.44
		2000 -9.10		1994 1.32		1988 16.61	1950 31.71
		2001 -11.89		2005 4.91		2006 15.80	1951 24.02
							1954 52.62
							1955 31.56
							1958 43.36
							1961 26.89
							1963 22.80
							1967 23.98
							1975 37.23
							1976 23.93
							1980 32.50
							1982 21.55
							1983 22.56
							1985 31.73
							1989 31.69
							1991 30.47
							1995 37.58
							1996 22.96
							1997 33.36
							1998 28.58
							1999 21.04
							2003 28.68

The S&P 500 Index has grown at or about its average rate of return of 10.30% only 5 times in 80 years. ⟶

8%<x<12%
1926 11.62
1959 11.96
1968 11.06
1993 10.08
2004 10.88

Source: UBS

To build a successful portfolio you need to know more than which stocks are risky. A statistical measurement called standard deviation comes into play. Standard deviation indicates how far from the mean (average) and investments historical performance has been. Two thirds (67%) of the time a specific asset class total return can be expected to fall within one standard deviation of the expected rate of return. As an example, if the asset class with one standard deviation of 8% and an expected rate of return of 10% should post returns which fall between 18% (eight plus 10) and 2% (10 minus eight) about two thirds of the time. A little complicated, isn't it? Perhaps your professional is really earning his or her keep. You now have a range your investment should fluctuate in 67% of the time.

As you can see from the exhibit below there are five major asset classes and the standard deviation of each. This higher standard deviation of stocks, both international and USA, relative to bonds and cash means their returns are more likely to swing dramatically during the short term. It is helpful to understand this is their normal behavior. This is especially the case with volatile small company stocks. Notice short term volatility associated with high standard deviation diminishes as the stock is owned for a longer period of time. For instance, investors who owned large cap stocks for 15 years or more have always had a positive return. *The Art of Investing* and Portfolio Management *page 46 Source: S&P Incert graph*

When we talked about a person's investment horizon in our risk tolerance questionnaire we purposely did this to determine whether stocks were an appropriate investment. The <u>longer</u> the time horizon for the investment, the more potential there is to use common stocks, because you may be able to afford some short-term ups and downs.

International stocks work much the same as U.S. stocks do far as volatility is concerned... The range of returns also narrows with the longer the investor holds the international stocks.

Since long-term government bonds have a lower standard deviation (9.4%) we know they will fluctuate less from year to year. Bonds, however, can still carry sizable risk which many average investors do not realize. One risk comes from rising interest rates which is an environment we are currently experiencing (i.e., 2014). It is especially hurtful for bonds with maturities of 10 years or more. Typically an interest rate rise of 1% (on a 10 year US Government bond) will result in a 9% decrease in the bond value (Source: JPMorgan, Guide to the Markets, 3Q/2013, page 32). Short-term and intermediate term bonds are less affected by interest rate fluctuations.

Many people feel the easy solution to volatility and diversification is adding long-term bonds to a stock portfolio; however, history shows long-term bonds do not add as much stability as we might hope. A better solution to reducing the volatility of a portfolio with stocks would be to add short or intermediate term bond issues.

Cash investments offer the lowest volatility, as measured by the standard deviation (2.3%) and not surprisingly the lowest long-term historical annualized return (3.3%). Source: S & P . While cash equivalents such as treasury bills and money market accounts are appealing for their stability, they simply cannot provide the growth needed to achieve an offset to inflation and may not reach the retirees goals over time.

At this point Ruth might interject into the conversation that a 3.3% historical annualized return on cash investments wouldn't be too bad over their lifetime since they had no volatility. Her point is a logical one. The problem comes when you take into consideration inflation and income taxes. As an example, if your income tax rate is 20%, your return is reduced from 3.3% to 2.64% (i.e., 3.3 x .20 = .66%; 3.3-.66=2.64% after tax return). If inflation has averaged 3.1% since 1926 you can see Ted and Ruth will be losing purchasing power every year after the inflation and taxes are taken into consideration (i.e., 3.1%-2.6 = -.5 purchasing power loss). This loss of purchasing power will not have much effect in the early years of their retirement; however, over a 20 year period their purchasing power will have been reduced by 50%(Source: Fidelity Advisors, American' Lifetime income challenge). They will be reducing their standard of living.

Building Block Number 3... Correlation Coefficients

Modern portfolio theory seeks to manage the risk and return of an entire portfolio, not just the individual components in it. Now that you have a good idea of the types of returns and risk each asset class delivers we can combine this knowledge with how they mix in a portfolio. Our goal is to combine the various asset classes in a way they will add the most value to the investment strategy and give the best possible return for the level of risk a person is comfortable taking.

A key word in the allocation process is 'lockstep'. We want to design a portfolio that is made up of asset classes that are **not** in lockstep with each other. In other words, they don't all move in the same direction at the same time. In this way, a negative return from one asset class in your portfolio can be offset by a positive return from another.

Correlation.

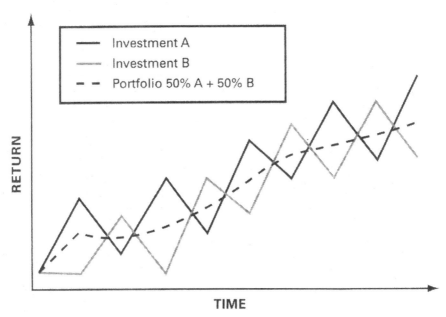

Correlation is the mathematical relationship between asset classes during an investment cycle. If two asset classes have a correlation of plus one, they are said to have perfect positive correlation. Their values will move simultaneously in the same direction. They are moving in 'lockstep'. If the assets have a correlation of -1, they have perfect negative correlation. Their prices therefore will move in exactly the opposite direction. The concept of modern portfolio theory is to team up classes of assets with negative correlation to each other so what causes one asset class to go up may cause the other to be flat or go down. Therefore, over time you receive an average rate of return from each. Let me give you a simple example. Suppose you own a ski lodge in the mountains. Six months of the year you are booming and six months of the year you are closed. If you bought another ski lodge you would have a plus one correlation... both lodges would be in lockstep. Instead of buying the second ski lodge, perhaps you purchase a swimming pool installation and service company. The swimming pool company would have a negative one correlation to the ski lodge (i.e., the swimming pool company will be doing business in the summer months) and would level out the revenue over the course of the year instead of having a period of great income and no income.

A investment example of low correlation at work combines common stock with bonds. It doesn't work perfectly, but, bonds tend to perform well during periods when stocks are suffering, and vice a versa. By combining stocks and bonds into your portfolio, you can achieve strong returns while lowering the portfolios over-all level of volatility/risk. Effective diversification accomplishes the objective of providing less volatility.

Don't make the mistake of combining two asset classes with high correlation. The S&P 500 and the Dow Jones have close to a plus one correlation; therefore, they would not provide effective diversification. Instead they are in lockstep. You might ask, "Why?" Didn't you tell me that we don't want to put all our eggs in one basket? Yes, I did. Remember though we want to have asset classes that are not highly correlated. The S&P 500 in the Dow Jones are made up of many of the same type of companies and so have a high degree of correlation... their prices almost always move in the same direction.

Are you getting the point? Advanced asset allocation is not simply concerned with dividing the assets up in any random manor. Instead, proper asset allocation focuses on dividing them up in effective ways using scientific research. If a person ignores effective correlation they could easily fall into the trap of dividing the money among categories moving in the same direction and therefore wind up with ineffective diversification which may result in big losses.

Correlation among major asset classes (1970–March 2007).

Asset Class	S&P 500	Treasury Bills	Long-Term Government Bond	U.S. Small Caps	Foreign Stocks (EAFE)
S&P 500	1.0000				
Treasury bills	−0.0280	1.0000			
Long-term government bonds	0.2441	0.0632	1.0000		
U.S. Small caps	0.7344	−0.0555	0.1142	1.0000	
Foreign Stocks (EAFE)	0.5529	−0.0627	0.1323	0.4432	1.0000

Source: Standard & Poors

Review the correlation among the different asset classes listed on the above chart. Do you see the negative correlation between some asset classes, such as long-term government bonds and foreign stocks (the foreign stocks are represented by MSCI EAFE Index). What does that mean? These asset classes will tend to move in opposite directions and provide effective diversification benefits if both are included in a portfolio. In contrast, the returns of international stocks follow the S&P 500's return somewhat closely and will provide a lesser degree of volatility reduction when the two asset classes are combined. You're probably thinking, "Wow, that was some pretty heavy stuff." You're 100% right. Understanding Modern Portfolio Theory and the three essential building blocks to effective asset allocation is heady stuff. They don't give the Nobel Peace Prize in Economics to just anyone. Dr. Markowitz, the father of Modern Portfolio Theory, began working on his theories in 1952 and not until 38 years later was he recognized with the Nobel Peace Prize. I purposely went into a lot of details on advanced asset allocation because I want you to understand there is more to it than looking at your 401(k) statement once a year and seeing which funds did the best and picking those for your next year's allocation. My suggestion is to team up with a professional who is competent in these areas. I'll give you my suggestions on determining their competency in a chapter to follow.

Chapter 8
Selecting a Financial Advisor

Ted and Ruth had a dilemma during those early months as they were making plans for their retirement. So many of the financial decisions during the years Ted worked for Sunoco were relatively automatic. The company had an excellent human resource and benefits department. His job afforded him most, if not all, of the areas to provide financial security for him and his family. By becoming an employee of Sunoco he was provided health insurance, life insurance, disability income insurance, a credit union, a pension plan, and a contributory retirement plan (i.e., 401k). Sure, he had to make some decisions when it came to each of these benefits (i.e., which investment accounts he should use for his contributory retirement plan, electing additional life insurance benefits, etc.), but the company had put it all in place with very little effort needed by him. Now, after working decades in an environment which took little effort or study by him he was going out on his own. His environment had been somewhat like the safety of a cocoon. Retirement means leaving the cocoon and all the support it provided.

Now he and Ruth had to make these decisions on their own.

In one of our early meetings Ted said to me, "Skip, I feel very nervous about making some of the decisions required of me once I leave the company. Do I spend a great deal of time becoming knowledgeable in investment types and allocations? Do I hire a professional to guide me in these very important and difficult decisions? If I hire a professional, how do I know they are competent and have my best interests at heart? What is the cost and am I getting a fair value? Part of me says I can do it myself and yet I don't really feel I can. If I made some wrong decisions my retirement safety net could be destroyed. Do you see why I feel overwhelmed?"

President Bill Clinton said it pretty appropriately, "I feel your pain". When we step back and look at all of the decisions to be made it is clear Ted has reason to feel overwhelmed. Perhaps he can do a good job of providing the answers to these questions himself. It simply means he should be very sober in approaching answers to the questions he and Ruth face. After spending almost five decades in the financial services industry I have developed some thoughts which will help Ted and Ruth decide if they can do it on their own or if they would benefit by hiring a financial adviser. After reading this chapter, you'll be armed with the most important questions to ask as you face the question of doing it yourself or hiring an adviser.

Have you ever heard the phrase 'timing is everything'? That certainly applies to the investment world. If you had asked most people during the 1980s and in 1990s if they needed a financial adviser and probably have told you, "I don't think so." The S&P 500 index gained an average of 15% per year during those years. Many people became callous to risk and felt the golden age of technology and information would carry the stock market for decades to come.

Many investors in such an environment couldn't imagine how a financial adviser was capable of adding value... much less why they should pay them. I remember stories of taxi drivers with laptops in the front seat of their cab doing day trading in the stock market. I have done financial plans for people who wanted to assume an annual return of 15% per year...they were offended I suggested a lesser rate.

We know now dreadful markets can occur rather abruptly and continue for years. The S&P 500 declined over 40% from 2000 through 2003 while the NASDAQ was down over 70%. That decline repeated itself again from November 2007 through March of 2009. This time it was called the 'credit crises'. Nearly two thirds of investors with assets of $10,000-$1,000,000 to invest experienced as much as a 50% reduction in the value of their portfolios. Thirty five percent suffered losses of more than 50%. What a tough way to be reminded investing is, in fact not easy, nor a game that is fun to play in our spare time.

Ted and Ruth lived through this time of astounding losses. Fortunately they were still employed and not having to draw on their retirement account. Can you see why Ted is concerned about managing his retirement account without professional help? He's not alone in seeking professional financial help. The exhibit below shows that nearly 90% of high net worth investors are currently expressing interest in working with financial professionals. That is up from just 37% in 1997. Timing is everything!

Strong demand for financial advice.

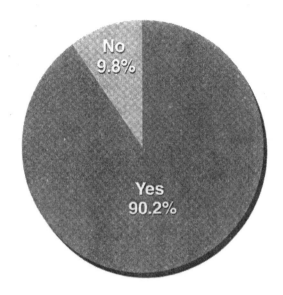

Source: Merrill Lynch Investment Managers, CEG Worldwide

Professor Otar said retirement is somewhat luck in addition to good planning. For instance, the people who were lucky to retire in 1982 had the good fortune to have a stock market that averaged 15% per year for the next 18 years. With the winds of the bull market behind you no one needed much help. Those retiring in 1929, 1973, 2000 or 2008 faced much tougher investment times.

After Ted brought up his concerns, both the cost of a financial adviser as well and the need, I suggested he be very introspective about his own investing habits, comfort, and skill level. "Ted," I said, "write down honest, unflinching answers to these questions."

1. In the past have I invested in a disciplined and rational manner? Have I invested in undervalued asset classes while reducing my exposure to high-flying areas...did I 'buying low and selling high?' (i.e., as my Dad always told me to do). Did I

let my emotions – greed, fear, and panic get the best of me and drive my portfolio decisions?

2. **Did** I have a strategy developed based on my long term objectives? Did I stick to my strategy when stock prices fell further and further? Did falling value cause me to abandon my plan? When the news was bad, did I sell or when things were great did I invest into the market bubble?

3. How much time am I willing to commit towards developing and maintaining an investment plan? Reading the business section of the newspaper is not sufficient study to monitor your plan.

4. Can I make the best decisions and then take action about asset allocation, investment selection, and rebalancing?

"Once you have answered these questions, you'll know whether you can do the job yourself or you need to hire a financial adviser."

What Are the Benefits Of Hiring a Financial Adviser?

After reviewing the questions I outlined for Ted, he looked at me soberly and said, "Skip, I don't think there is any question Ruth and I need the help of an investment advisor. Help me to understand what do I get for my money." I was amazed at Ted's openness. "Ted and Ruth", I said, "that's an easy one for me. Advisors offer these important benefits:

Time is first. In order to do an effective job you must spend significant amounts of effort and time. These are some of the items to be addressed... developing your goals, determining your risk/return comfort level, developing an Investment Policy Statement (IPS), design an efficient portfolio, and perform ongoing monitoring, and rebalancing. My experience has taught me most people would rather spend their time with their families or doing the fun activities important to them and have someone else do these time consuming activities.

Skill level comes in second. Most investors simply do not have the level of skill needed to be truly effective. This is not to say individual investors are not capable of achieving success. Some are very successful. The fact is advanced training and market knowledge are key differences between investors who obtain their goals and those who fall short of their goals. Most investors are not willing to take the time required to gain this knowledge.

Discipline is third. Behavioral finance studies reveal emotions can be an overwhelming force when it comes to decisions about money. Studies show the brain is hard wired to avoid loss. The quote, "investors make wrong decisions at the wrong time for all the wrong reasons" has a great deal of truth to it. When our own money is on the line we are emotionally wired to making poor financial choices. Those poor financial decisions might be buying into a market bubble or selling at a loss when negative news is predominant. By contrast, professional advisors who are devoted to serving their client's best interest have systems in place to consistently help them make objective, rational decisions. They are not immune to the emotional market environments but their <u>process and systems</u> help to keep the emotional knee jerk reactions in check.

Finding a Good Advisor

In my opinion, your financial advisor should be the quarterback in the process of "getting your financial house in order". You should be counting on your adviser to help you manage your entire financial future. You're paying the advisor to do it correctly.

Unfortunately, a significant number of professional advisors in the financial service field do not serve their investors as well as they should.

A 2003 study asked the question, "How satisfied are you with your advisor?" Below are the disappointing results:

Poor rating............3.6%
Fair rating............69.7%
Excellent............26.7%

Source: Russ Alan Prince and Brett Van Bortel, "The Millionaire's Advisor' New York, Institutional Investor News, 2003

In my experience financial advisers can be divided into two broad categories... single discipline planners and multi-discipline planner. The single discipline planner typically does the majority of their work within the confines of a single financial discipline. For instance, their main source of revenue comes from specializing in one of the following fields: life insurance, real estate, stock brokerage sales, or annuity sales. Many may have licenses in the various disciplines, but if you look at their 1040 income tax statement you'd find that 80% to 90% of their income comes from a single discipline. There is certainly nothing wrong with being a single discipline professional. My concern is the objectivity involved. Too often the single disciplined professional will see their product as the solution for every client's needs. It is like the old saying, "If you're a hammer then you will see everything as a nail".

The multi-discipline planner is typically licensed and registered in all of the disciplines mentioned above. The qualifying point is the multidiscipline planner works from a consultative approach. Their focus should be on solving problems you may have with no preconceived product in mind. They are not trained to focus on specific products or investment vehicles. Instead they address the full range of your financial needs. They should begin the process with no preconceived notions of what you need. Once a painstaking evaluation of a person's needs is made then recommendations are made.

Consultative advisors work with their clients in a fundamentally different way than product-orientated advisors. Consultative advisers should use a defined process for asking a series of questions to uncover goals and objectives. The knowledge is used to formulate a comprehensive solution. I call this part of the process a 'financial physical'. Their goal is to develop a deeper relationship with their clients allowing them to build and maintain superior overall investment and financial plans. Typically, the consultative advisor will ask what the attorney will call 'discovery questions'. Discovery questions lead to the recommendations needed to solve the goals uncovered.

Five Essential Qualifications

Remember our discussion of the first meeting with Ted and Ruth. During the discussion Ted made it clear that he had already visited with another financial advisor and planned on talking with at least one more advisor before making a decision. I replied, "Ted and Ruth, planning for your retirement is an important decision. You would be foolish not to evaluate several people before you make a decision. Don't make the mistake of working with someone simply because you feel 'comfortable' with them or you feel you can 'trust' them."

As you begin your search for an advisor, keep these five criteria in mind as you evaluate each of your potential advisors. The advisor you choose should measure up in all five areas.

1. A Registered Investment Advisor

There are many professional designations and titles, and I believe your advisor should have one of these designations: Certified Financial Planner (CFP), Chartered Financial Analyst (CFA), and Chartered Financial Consultant (ChFC).

We also strongly recommend that you work only with professionals who are formally registered with the Securities and Exchange Commission (SEC) and FINRA as Registered Investment Advisor (RIA). There is a simple reason for this recommendation. Registered Investment Advisors have a legal fiduciary responsibility to provide their clients with the highest possible standard of care. As a fiduciary, an RIA is required by law to always look out for the client's best interest and to completely and objectively disclose all important information in his or her dealings with the client. By contrast, a stock or annuity sales person is not legally required to always work in your best interest.

Instead, a person just selling a product is held to a lesser standard of care which may create a conflict of interest.

As a form of extra disclosure, the RIA is required to provide the client with a Federal document known as an ADV. This document outlines the services they provide, how they are compensated, if they have been sanctioned or disciplined by the SEC or FINRA and any outside business relationships. The ADV is to be provided to you early in the working process.

2. The advisor is consultative

I discussed the benefits of a multi-disciplined advisor versus a single-disciplined advisor a few pages earlier. Everything said there applies in this discussion of using only a consultative advisor.

3. The advisor uses a fee-based structure instead of commissions

Commissions bring into every transaction a potential conflict of interest. Have you ever wondered whether your financial representative was suggesting you buy or sell a particular security because it was in your best interest or because they were making a commission? The only reason a question might come up in your mind is because a commission will be paid on a purchase or sale transaction. Please understand I'm not saying commission people will act in their own self interest. There are many honorable and ethical financial advisors who work on a commission basis. My point is when commissions are involved in a sale or purchase there is an inherent conflict of interest.

On the other hand a fee-based advisor may receive an advisory fee based on the portfolio's assets value. There is not an upfront sales charges. If the account is moved, the fee ends; therefore, the advisor has a vested interest to continue to provide service and advise. If not they run the risk of losing the account. The range is typically between .50% and 1.75% (i.e., the fee is based on the size of asset under management). A purchase or sale within the account has no impact on the compensation of the fee-based advisor. I like to think of the fee-based advisor as being on the same side of the table as the client. If the client's account goes up in value the fee-based advisor is rewarded because the compensation will increase. If the clients account goes down in value the fee-based advisor suffers just as the client does because his compensation will go down. Therefore, a fee-based advisor has an incentive to continue providing the best advice.

4. The advisor uses an excellent process

Many people choose an advisor because they like them or they trust them. Liking and trusting your advisor are important; however, it doesn't mean the client is receiving thorough and effective guidance. Personally I would not work with someone I did not like or trust. Developing an effective retirement plan together with "getting your financial house in order" is a daunting task which may continue for a person's lifetime. The consequences of the plan failing are colossal. Good intentions are not enough to ensure success.

Ted and Ruth, as well as all those who are entering a retirement planning phase of their life, need to identify and work with only those advisors who deliver the highest level of skill and optimal resources at each stage of the investment process. There are six steps in the investment process. Any advisor you choose to work with should use a process addressing all of six steps. The six steps in the investment process are:

1) a comprehensive financial analysis (your goals, risk tolerance, return objectives, time horizon, and so on)
2) the development of an Investment Policy Statement (IPS) which identifies all elements of the investment plan acting as a roadmap designed to keep you on track when difficult markets arise
3) a minimum of one professional portfolio strategist to evaluate and monitor all asset allocation decisions and the various investment managers (Proper asset allocation is a critical issue to address being key to returns.)

4) multiple investment vehicles including mutual funds, stocks,exchange traded funds (ETFs), private accounts, REITS, alternative investments,and tax-deferred annuities tailored around your investable assets and preferred investment style
5) a disciplined system for regular portfolio rebalancing to enable you to methodically and unemotionally "buy low and sell high"
6) a planned method of monitoring and evaluating your portfolios, your tax situation and your progress toward your most important goals

5. You Should Be Comfortable with the Advisor

Life is too short to be dealing with people we don't like. As an advisor I've 'fired' some bossy, difficult clients who just didn't seem to value my opinion. As a client you also have the same option to 'fire' an advisor who makes you uncomfortable or you question their competence. It is your money and you have the right to decide with whom to work.

When Ted and I first met I asked Ted, "When you're evaluating an advisor ask yourself if you can work with this person? Will you enjoy your meetings and other interactions? Do I get the feel this advisor will work in my best interest and help me meet my goals?"

This last criterion is a 'softer' issue than the other four which have been covered in the last few pages; however, you may be working with this person for many, many years so this last item should not be overlooked.

Chapter 9

Wealth Transfer Process...Why is it so hard?

The steps Ted and Ruth have taken since our first meeting have been outstanding. Look at what they have accomplished:

- They have developed a retirement strategy which has given them more peace of mind and assurance of meeting their goals
- They have reviewed their income and potential estate taxes and have taken steps to reduce them.
- They have reviewed all of their insurance coverage to ensure no gaps or incorrect beneficiaries.
- They have developed an effective asset allocation strategy to fit their current retirement stage of life. That strategy is now focused on asset protection and producing income.

The next area to be addressed is estate planning. Most agree this is an important area to focus on yet it is so often neglected. Procrastination is probably the biggest obstacle to overcome. It is human nature to feel we still have more time. Senator Robert S. Kerr, the late senior United States Senator from Oklahoma, died with a newly written, unsigned trust lying on the bedside table of his hospital room. He was recuperating from a heart attack. Most professionals agree by signing the trust he could have saved his estate literally millions of dollars in death taxes. Why didn't he sign? Who knows, but probably because he felt he had a few more days to get it done. That's an extreme case yet most of us delay in getting our will or trust put into effect or updated.

Another reason many of us wait is the confusion, mystique, and myths involved with estate planning... what are my options, what do all these terms mean, what is the correct and best way to leave my money to the children, etc. For many, the easiest way to address these difficult questions is to procrastinate, thinking there will be a better time in the future.

Transferring our Assets is a Challenge...the outcome of your will and trust

The reality is we cannot take any of our possessions with us when we die. These decisions are tough since they are so final. These are some of the challenges you face while planning your will and trust (i.e., the eventual transfer of assets):

➢ providing for your spouse is a way to care for her needs yet not burdening her with financial decisions with which she may have no experience
➢ helping your children and grandchildren
➢ avoiding family conflicts and sibling jealousies which could split the family
➢ dealing with in-laws... sons-in-law, daughters-in-law, stepchildren... especially if you do not respect or trust any of them
➢ managing expectation of children and spouses
➢ providing for charities and ministries you support while deciding the amount to give
➢ accepting the reality of your death
➢ talking with family about this difficult subject may be uncomfortable
➢ coming to agreement with your spouse regarding what is to be done...how funds are to be divided
➢ learning complex legal and financial matters, such as wills trust estate taxes, etc.
➢ desiring to control your assets from the grave
  (Source: Splitting Heirs, page 35)

No wonder Senator Robert S. Kerr procrastinated. Most of us tend to follow in his procrastinating footsteps.

Source: <u>Splitting Heirs, Giving your Money and Things to your Children Without Ruining Their Lives, Ronald Blue</u>

Let's look back in on Ted and Ruth as they wrestle with some of these important decisions. My basic question to them was, "What do you want to happen to your assets when you both are gone?" Ruth replied, "We want to protect the value of our assets so there is no burden on the children for our medical, nursing home and death expenses. We also would like to have some money to pass on to our children. Since we have children from different marriages we definitely want to alleviate any misunderstanding about our wishes and the division of our properties." Ted chimed in, "As you know, Susie, our youngest child, was born with Down's syndrome and we're concerned how to provide for her once Ruth and I are gone. There are no easy solutions."

Every family must be treated individually when it comes to estate planning. Their special needs must be addressed. After decades of reviewing wills, trusts, and estate plans, I find many of the plans have not met the goals of those for whom the plan was developed.

There are many causes. Perhaps there has been no planning done at all. Too often, assuming there is a will or trust document, it was done in a 'cookie cutter' fashion not really addressing the unique needs of the particular family.

These are my goals for this chapter:

- to demystify the estate planning process
- to give you simple steps on how you can develop a plan to meet the unique needs of your family
- to motivate you into action, like the Nike ad 'Just Do It'

Rather than spew out terms and definitions I would like to use the Dunleavy family as a case study in developing an efficient and effective estate plan. To do that, you will need some information on Ted and Ruth's family and their goals. Please understand I am not an attorney and am not giving legal advice. An estate planning attorney is necessary to draw up the proper documents for your situation.

Family background:

There are four children. This is a second marriage for both Ted and Ruth. They each had one child by a previous marriage, and they have two children together. Ted is 64 while Ruth is age 60.

Ruth's first husband was a president of a regional company with 80 employees. Ruth and her first husband moved to Oklahoma from the Northeastern section of the United States. After locating in Oklahoma, her husband developed a brain tumor and died within a year of diagnosis. The shock of losing her husband was overwhelming. As an example, Ruth went months without opening the mail which caused the electricity and water to be turned off twice because of unpaid bills. This was a dark time of confusion, depression and despair.

Learning about his wife's experience of losing her husband to cancer had a profound effect on Ted. He developed a strong relationship with God after he and Ruth married. He actively gives to charities and to his church. His plans are to continue these contributions at his death.

Ruth has worked as a teacher for the last 20 years. She, also, is about to retire. She will be covered under the Oklahoma Teachers Retirement System. Ruth's life revolves around the children. Although they are all grown she is still very close to them and involved in their lives. For each of the last four years the families have all gathered together for a family vacation. In the last two years they have gone to Yellowstone National Park and Park City, Utah. Ted and Ruth paid for the kids' trip expenses. One of the reasons Ted has hesitated to retire is the fear he will not be able to afford these trips which he feels are the other 'extras'. Ruth feels the same way. Their investable assets total $850,000.

The children:

Ronnie, Ted's oldest son by a previous marriage, is age 41 and married to Connie. They have two children named Bobby and Sam. Ronnie is a property and casualty insurance agent and earns a good income. The children are 16 and 13. Connie works part-time for an architectural firm as an interior designer. They have never asked or received financial help from Ted or Ruth. Connie is from Korea. She and Ronnie met while they were in college. Connie's parents still live in Korea; therefore, there is an extra need for security in the case of the death of Ronnie.

Julia is Ruth's daughter by her first marriage. She is 35 and divorced with two children, ages 14 and 9. Julia works for the City of Tulsa as an assistant to the Mayor. She gets little help from her ex-husband in the way of child support. She relies on financial help from Ted and Ruth on a regular basis.

Hank is the first child Ted and Ruth had together. He is 28 and single. He has never been married and works as an auditor for Marriott Hotels in Dallas, Texas. He has always been financially responsible.

Susie, their second child, is 20 and still living at home. Ruth was 40 when she became pregnant with Susie. Suzie was born with Down syndrome and will always need financial assistance.

Not such an unusual American family. Before giving you some of the thoughts Ted and Ruth should consider, let's talk about the three basics of estate planning:

- the basic steps in the estate planning process
- types of wills and trusts
- choosing the estate planning team

Basic steps in the estate planning process:

- Choose your team: Choose, as needed, your attorney, tax professional, financial planner, trust officer and planned giving specialist. The size and complexity of your estate is a determining factor of your team. Typically the financial planner is the quarterback of the team. He should have developed the most thorough understanding of your goals and assets.
- Gather information: Completing a data form serves to list your goals and objectives, shows names, ages, assets and liabilities, desired heirs, goals and objectives. You may have already done this with your financial planner.

- Analyze data: A good way to start the process is to pretend you died yesterday. What happens to your estate, your business, and your family? Who gets what and how much? For most of us it would be a mess! What if you die ten years from now? Your team analyzes the data to provide you with the results of taxes due and assets available for distribution to the family and charitable groups.
- Team recommendations: The next step is to review the suggestions made by the team to accomplish your goals and avoid shortcomings.
- Decision and implementation: After reviewing the recommendations, decide upon the plan you feel best fits your needs and goals. Implement the plan by signing the essential documents (wills and trust), purchase needed insurance, change investments as necessary, update beneficiaries, etc.
- Periodic review: Because the world and your situation are constantly changing, we recommend a review at least every five years.

(Source: Splitting Heirs)

Types of wills and trusts:

Let me again note my concern, too often the various documents are filled out prematurely before the various issues outlined above are fully addressed. Wills and trust documents are simply tools and techniques to accomplish an objective just as specific prescription drugs are tools to help the body heal. Does it make sense to be recommending a specific prescription drug before the medical sickness has been diagnosed? This is specifically why I feel so many wills and trust are not drawn with the goals, values, and desires of the estate owner. Too often the estate owner does not take the time and effort to think through this difficult process of deciding what they really want to happen. The various documents below should only be drafted after deciding what you really want to do. In my opinion the documents should only be drafted by an attorney specializing in estate planning law is a complex area of law. A mistake might invalidate the entire plan.

These are, in my opinion, the most common documents to consider as you develop your plan. My purpose is to give you some of the basics without boring you. This is a complex area and I am giving brief and simple definitions of these documents.

Basic will: The simple or basic will generally provide all assets go directly to the surviving spouse, children or other heirs. I often refer to it as the "I love you" will. It can be appropriate for people with few assets. These assets are subject to probate.

Will with contingent trust: Often, couples who have minor children will pass everything to the spouse, if living, and if not, to a trust for their minor children until they reach a more mature age. These assets are subject to probate.

Pour over will: This will is generally used in conjunction with a living trust. It is designed to make sure any assets not titled in the trust will automatically 'pour into the trust' upon the person's death. These assets that pour over into the trust avoid probate.

Tax wise trust: This is a technique used in larger estates to avoid death taxes (i.e., estate taxes). It may be called a credit shelter trust. It provides for lifetime benefits, from the credit shelter portion of the trust, to the surviving spouse. The assets in the credit shelter trust avoid being included in the survivor's estate at his or her subsequent death.

Revocable Living Trust: One of the main purposes of this trust is to avoid probate and provide a smooth transition of assets at the owner's death. Normally, the surviving spouse has full control of both the principal and the income. If there are surviving or dependent children who lack experience in financial and investment matters, the trust can also manage the assets for those beneficiaries who are not yet ready to inherit the assets outright.

Revocable Living Trust Credit Shelter Provision: This is used in larger taxable estates to ensure that both spouses receive their estate credit exemption. The trust is also designed to avoid probate. In 2014 a living credit shelter trust could pass $5,340,000 per spouse to children and other heirs without Federal death taxes (assuming a married couple used this type of trust).

The estate planning team:

Estate planning is complicated. Various professional disciplines may be required to address areas that include law, insurance, taxation, business continuation, estate, gift and income taxes. As you can imagine it would be difficult for one person to be an expert in all areas; therefore, an estate planning team may be assembled. As with other teams a captain or quarterback should be in charge. Since the financial planner has gathered and worked with the client on all of these areas they are normally the best candidate to quarterback the team however, anyone of the estate planning team may act as the quarterback. The team may consist of some or all of the following:

Estate planning attorney... probate, death taxes, and administration expenses can run into thousands and perhaps millions of dollars. Although most attorneys can draft a basic will, I feel it is critical to have a specialist in estate planning law draft your will and trust instruments. This is too complicated and specialized an area to take a chance using a general practioner.

Tax professional... Federal law may require the filing of an estate tax return (i.e., IRS form 706) within nine months of death. This form is confusing and complicated; therefore you may be well advised to consult with a tax profession. During the estate planning development the tax professional may be needed to comment on property values or the taxation upon the sale of assets.

Financial planner... typically a financial planner has been involved in the creation and preservation of your wealth. If that is the case information on your current assets, your family, your goals and plans to pass on your assets has been gathered. Many times the financial planner can oversee the team to make sure no area is left uncovered and to review on a regular basis any changes that may need to be made.

Trust administrator... you may choose to have a relative act as the executive of your will or of your trust. The other option is to select a corporate fiduciary (i.e, a bank or a trust company) to provide this role. If you choose the corporate trustee you may consider involving them in the development of your estate plan. A corporate trustee will normally charge a fee to administer the trust.

Why most estate planning is flawed

Have you heard the phrase, 'garbage in, garbage out'? Typically we are referring to computers when we use that term. In reality, it can refer to a number of things in life. A child brought up in a dysfunctional home may have with a negative slant on life. You may be wondering how this applies to estate planning. Isn't developing an estate plan along with the documents to carry out plan pretty cut and dry? For instance, I tell my attorney the information about my family and he draws the proper trust. What could be dangerous about the process?

The danger comes from too much time spent on the tools and techniques (i.e., the documents) and too little time spent on the thinking and analyzing of your situation and what you want to accomplish. Let me explain.

The tools, techniques, and strategies of estate planning are completed by the documents. Before implementing the documents consider carefully what you want to do and why you want to do it. I find this is the area too often neglected.

The 'what' you want to happen and the 'why' you want it to happen involves thinking about your values, your goals, your passions, and your interest. This is the blueprint for what you want your estate plan to do.

In building your dream house you wouldn't consider hiring a contractor to go out and start building without a well drawn plan. Hours upon hours are needed to determine all of the major and minor details... the size of the rooms, the entry way, the flow, the colors, the carpeting, the window placements, etc. All of this is the 'what and why' work. Only after you have developed the blueprint do you go to the contractor and break ground. In my estimation, developing an estate plan should proceed in the same order. All the challenging questions that were raised on pages earlier in the book must be answered for this blueprint to reflect your wishes and values. Too often the will or trust is drawn without the true wishes of the client being accomplished. The document may involve all the fine points of the law; however it may not address your deep seated thoughts and desires. Read carefully the following paragraphs, because this is the heart of the matter.

Most likely you have been considering a will or a trust for some time before finally taking the step to contact the attorney. We have a general idea of what we would like to accomplish but the 'blueprint' is only sketchy. Sure, we know we want to provide for the care of your spouse, and after your spouse dies the children are to receive what's left. But does this blueprint reflect your values, your unique family needs, and your goals? The attorney's job is not to develop the blueprint for you. His job is to take your blueprint, be it detailed or sketchy, and use the best tools and techniques to accomplish what the blueprint gives him. The attorney gets paid for drawing the document not for developing your blueprint.

Ted and Ruth currently have a will and trust which provide all the assets to the surviving spouse at the first death. At the second death, the assets will flow equally to the children. Pretty standard arrangement, wouldn't you agree? Now let's look at their specific situation and see if the above arrangements take into consideration Ted and Ruth's values, goals, missions, and passions. These are the questions their properly thought out blueprint would provide.

- If Ted dies first, Ruth will inherit approximately $850,000 plus $200,000 of life insurance proceeds. How will Ruth manage that money? Is she comfortable making financial decisions over such a large sum of money? Who would be the best to help Ruth with these investment and financial decisions? Would a corporate trustee be helpful to her or is there a trusted friend or child to provide the help?
- Ted and Ruth have provided for family vacations, for the family as a whole to come together, over the last four years. If Ted dies first does their plan provide for money to continue the family vacations in the future?

- Ted and Ruth have been active in tithing 10% to charities and their church. The current plan does not provide for any gift at his or her death. Didn't our case study mention he had a desire to give at his death? Perhaps addressing this in the estate documents provides an opportunity to share their values with the children and grandchildren.

- How much should be given to the children when Ted and Ruth are both gone? Should it be divided equally amongst the children. Should more be given to children with more need? Should there be some money left over that can be given to a charity or their church?

- Are all the children capable of handling a lump sum of money at the death of their mom or dad? Should there be different plans of distribution for each child taking into consideration their past abilities to handle money wisely? Would it be better for the children to receive their inheritance as an income rather than a lump sum?

- How should the money be divided between the children? Studies show women feel the money should be divided evenly, even though some of the children may be in a greater need. Our case study shows that Ronnie has never taken any financial help from his folks and he is somewhat financially independent. On the other hand, Julia, divorced and raising two children by herself, has needed help on a consistent basis. Hank has no family responsibility. Susie is living at home and will always be dependent on her folks for financial assistance. Would Ted and Ruth be out of line to provide more of an inheritance to the two children who need more help? How would mom and dad explain this arrangement to the children? Would a difference in inheritance cause a rift amongst the children after the parents have died? If mom and dad provide financial assistance for Susie, will that cut off any state or federal assistance for which she might be eligible?

- Should Ted and Ruth have a family meeting to explain to the children their estate distribution plans? This meeting could include how the assets would be divided between the children, why they are divided that way, and how much they might be giving to charities. If they don't have the family meeting will the children hug or fight after the second parent dies? My experience is there is always a family meeting, but too often one 'chair (i.e., Mom or Dad's) is vacant' when the attorney explains the will. Wouldn't it be better for Mom and Dad to explain their thinking to the children than have an attorney read a document?

- All of the above questions are what I call the 'what and why' questions. They are part of the blueprint needing to be totally explored and developed before the last meeting with the attorney and the document is inked. In my estimation, these questions are the most difficult part of the estate planning process. Unfortunately they are the most critical part and yet the part most left out of the estate planning process.

Financial Independence and its role in estate planning

Your financial independence number was addressed earlier and it plays a role in effective estate planning? Let's review again the concept of a person's financial independence number. Obviously, what represents financial independence for one family can be totally different for another. Your financial independence number is the amount of assets required for the couple or individual to live their normal lifestyle without running out of money during their lifetime. Our calculations will take into consideration a reasonable rate of return on investments, inflation, taxes, and potential additional unforeseen emergencies.

Financial independence occurs when enough assets have accumulated so adequate income will be provided for the rest of the individual's life or the rest of the lives of a couple. I call this the 'number'. Once you know what your 'financial independence number' is, you can determine if you have excess assets. In fact, when Ted and Ruth and I were discussing this he asked, "Skip, what difference does it make if I know there is excess of assets Ruth and I own. Doesn't that just give us additional safety?" The answer is definitely yes. You have additional safety. Knowing Ted has additional assets also allows him a latitude of options. The excess of assets provides the ability to make gifts, without worrying about running out of money. For those who have children and grandchildren it can be a liberating opportunity knowing they can help their loved ones and knowing it is from their excess funds.

As an illustration, recently I worked with a retired doctor living in Arkansas. He had an estate of approximately $3.8 million. He and his wife were in their mid-70s, in good health and interested in helping their children, grandchildren and charitable missions they supported. During our conversation he said, "My wife and I would really love to give substantially more to help with our grandchildren's education. We also are quite involved in a number of ministries. The problem is we just don't know how much money we need to live the rest of our lives. We're concerned we might run out of money". Not an unreasonable concern, wouldn't you agree?

Let's assume their financial independence number is $2.6 million to provide for their lifestyle until they are both gone.

Our suggestion is to build in a layer of additional assets for added safety.

This couple's 'excess wealth' is $1,200,000. Over $1,000,000 is potentially available to help their children, grandchildren or charitable missions during their lifetime. Instead of the money being passing at death, they will get the pleasure of seeing their loved ones and charities use, enjoy and benefit from it.

How Big Is My Wealth Bucket?

Most people do not think of themselves as being in the wealthy category. Somebody else is wealthy. Most of us the think we are average Americans regardless of the amount of wealth accumulated. As we end this section on estate planning, I recommend you take a moment and pull out a blank sheet of paper to see how much wealth you may have available during your lifetime and after your death. Simply input the approximate value of your different assets. You will also need to add in any unrealized money which may be available later, such as the life insurance to be paid at your death or future inheritances. For instance, assume you have one living brother and your ailing mother has named the two of you to share equally in her estate. Her house and C.D.s are worth approximately $400,000. You cannot count this money as your assets now, but it can be added in to your estimated wealth transferred to you at a later date. This will help you see how much might be eventually under your control

Assets That May Some Day Be Transferred

QUANTIFYING YOUR WEALTH TO TRANSFER

Wealth—Available Now:

Cash on hand and checking account	$ _____
Money market funds	_____
CDs	_____
Savings accounts	_____
401(k) and other retirement plans from your company	_____
IRAs	_____
Pension & profit sharing	_____
Mutual funds	_____
Bonds	_____
Equity in your home	
(market value less remaining mortgage balance)	_____
Land (market value)	
Business valuation (market value)	_____
Rental property	_____
Real estate—farm, lots, etc.	_____
Limited partnerships	_____
Boat, camper, tractor, etc.	_____
Automobiles	_____
Furniture and personal property (estimated market value)	_____
Coin and stamp collections, antiques	_____
Receivables from others	_____
Other:_____	_____
Other:_____	_____

Total Wealth Available Now $ _____

Unrealized Wealth—Available at or After Death

Life insurance proceeds upon your death	_____
Estimated inheritances you may receive later	_____

Total of Unrealized Wealth $ _____

Additional "What and Why Thinking"

All of these concepts I have brought up have to be blended with the individual's view of money and possessions. Please understand I certainly do not have the answers. We all get our philosophies from different sources and mine is built on 50 years of experience, training, and what I consider Biblical truth. The Bible teaches God owns everything. We are only temporary stewards of the property in our possession. A steward is <u>given authority</u> but not ownership of the property... we are to manage the property for the owner. In my thinking God is the owner.

As we wrap up the material involving estate planning I would like to end with four additional questions for you to consider. These are questions that dig into the heart of a person's values.

Who owns it?

The ownership of your assets, for an American, is cut and dry. Why of course you own it, you control it. However, the Christian's answer may be different. Stewardship is an interesting concept we don't hear much about in everyday life. A steward is a manager, an agent, a trustee, a servant of the actual owner of the property. The steward has management or supervision over the property. The steward must handle the property in the manner he or she perceives the owner would approve. If God is the owner and we are only temporary stewards of the property then our decisions regarding what is done with it takes on a new direction. Do you see the purpose in answering the question in your own mind of 'who owns it?'

How much is enough?

Again this question typically does not arise in our normal thinking. The normal thinking is always 'more is better'. We super size our French fries and our cold drinks. We want more horsepower in our automobiles. We buy bigger houses although our children have moved away. We have investable assets valued at $1 million and we want them to grow to $2 million. Once at $2 million we want the $2 million to grow to $4 million and so on. In the book of Ecclesiastics, from the Bible, there is a Scripture which basicly says, "More is never enough". For all these reasons it is important for us to decide how much is enough? What is our finish line? How much do I need for financial independence?

Who is the next steward?

My belief is God owns it all and we are only his temporary steward. When you are gone who should the next steward be?

Is the next steward prepared?

Tough assignments require wisdom. Wisdom is knowledge applied to life. Is the next steward ready for the wealth that you plan to pass on? Keep in mind the next steward might be your child, your grandchild or a charity. Are they prepared to be the next steward? If not, what can you do to help them acquire knowledge and wisdom about the proper management and stewardship of these assets?

Wisdom plays a part in building wealth; however, wealth rarely builds wisdom. A heavy truth to bear in mind while pondering the division the assets accumulated over a lifetime.

Chapter 10
Your Family Meeting

The final step in the 'Getting Your Financial House In Order' doesn't fit younger families.

The family meeting fits mature families who have gone through the estate planning process.

Ted and Ruth were in recently for their quarterly review. We have worked together for several years now and our meetings are more like a family reunion than a business session. As the session ended I asked Ted and Ruth if there were any other issues or concerns. Ted replied, "This isn't a concern, but I wanted to report to you Ruth and I have just completed a total review and revision of our estate plan. We worked with the attorney you recommended, Erin Donovan. We have nothing but the highest compliments for her work. The time we spent with you discussing our values, family needs and goals was so helpful. We took what we gathered from you and added the input from Erin. The combination of both helped us to develop a plan which truly accomplishes what is important to us."

After hearing some of the specifics of their plan I asked, "Have you set a time for a family meeting to discuss your estate plans with the children? After working so hard on developing your wealth transfer, if you fail to complete the family meeting, the impact of your plans will be reduced and may cause harm to those in your family. It is hard to talk about money and even harder to talk about money and death but it is a critical step in this whole process." As you might imagine, the next question to come out of Ruth's mouth was, "Why do we need to share our estate plan with our kids?"

There is always a family meeting to discuss the estate plan. The question is whether you will be alive to attend. Where do you prefer to share your transfer plans with your children... around the kitchen table or the coffin? Who can better discuss your motivations, hopes, desires, and blessings with your family; you or your lawyer reading your will?

By getting everyone in the family on the same page surprises can be avoided . The author of <u>The Prayer of Jabez</u>, Bruce Wilkinson, suggests many times there is a 'coping gap' for heirs. He defines the coping gap as the expectations of the heirs being at a different level than the reality. The difference between the expectation and the reality is the coping gap.

Perhaps you have an adult child who is expecting an inheritance of $400,000. You provide $300,000 to a charity you choose which means child only receives $100,000. That is a $300,000 coping gap. That child could have a very difficult time excepting such a difference from their expectations. Hard feelings can be created.

It can also work the other way. Perhaps the children have no idea what mom and dad have accumulated. They assume they will receive $50,000 and to their surprise their inheritance is $500,000. What a pleasant surprise to them, but it still may be a confusing time.

Coping gaps happen. You may wonder how to avoid them so your children have the right expectations. As with many problems, talk is the best solution. Perhaps one of my best suggestions in this book is to discuss your plans now with your kids. It might mean the difference between your kids hugging each other or not talking to each other.

I saw the coping gap in reality recently. A long time friend came from a family with five children. I had always admired the closeness of the family. The children had grown to be successful adults and moved out of the immediate area where their family farm was located. It was a large farm with approximately 500 acres. They raised wheat and cattle. All of the children gathered on many of the weekends throughout the year to continue a joint venture of working the cattle and the wheat. When the last parent died, the farmhouse was left to the oldest son who lived in a nearby town. The other four children felt betrayed when the oldest brother would not share the house with them. This close-knit family, who had worked together in the fields for many years, was split. A family meeting to discuss the parent's plans and their reasoning could have prevented this split.

As I said earlier there is always be family conference. Too often there is an empty chair at the conference because daddy just died. Wouldn't it be better to have the conference prior to the parent's death.

The conference gives an opportunity to share transfer decisions, values, family philosophies, etc. Parents, children, and grandchildren can understand each other better and learn from each other.

In addition it is a great opportunity for mom and dad to share their values of thriftiness, hard work, and patience...the traits which helped them to have a successful life. It is also a excellent time to share their thoughts on regarding finances and debt.

As a parent, I feel it my responsibility to pass on to my children the lessons I have learned in life. As the children mature and leaves home it's more difficult to have opportunities to pass on these lessons. Family meetings provide this opportunity. We have the opportunity to really talk and to listen to each other. I mentioned this earlier, but it is too important not to repeat, Ron Blue, a financial planner and friend said it best, "Wisdom may bring wealth, but wealth will rarely bring wisdom." Assuming you agree, wisdom should be transferred to those we love before wealth.

Planning Your Family Conference

The family meeting gives us continuing opportunities to discuss our plans and to pass on the wisdom we have acquired. Communication opens the way to greater understanding. Will you be comfortable discussing and developing wealth transfer plans with your children? Probably not. Will your children be comfortable bringing up issues with you?

I know I was not comfortable asking my dad about his financial plans. I did not want to seem nosey or greedy. The result...nothing was ever discussed. When he died after an extended illness there were problems I might have been able to help avoid.

Parents certainly have the right to do with their assets as they please. The family conference gives a forum so they can explain their issues, while all parties are present, rather than after the death. The family members are given opportunities to ask questions. This is an opportunity to increase family harmony and the potential to avoid bitterness generated over money issues.

113

A family conference can be as simple as the parents sitting down with the children and explaining what they are doing financially. The meeting may be around the kitchen table or it may be a weekend retreat. The most effective conference uses a moderator. Typically the moderator is a trusted financial advisor and/or an attorney. This may be an outline of key items for a family meeting:

Communicate about your specifics plans. As we look at Ted and Ruth's situation there may be money allocated for charities and the inheritance between the children may be unequal. Many people improperly believe their estate should be split equally among the children. Ted, as a Christian, may feel money should be left to those who have demonstrated good stewardship principles. We all have seen the examples of leaving money to someone who does not have wisdom, the results can be devastating. Hopefully a discussion of these areas can lead to improvements in our children or grandchildren's ability to handle money effectively.

Communicate about lifetime giving. Ted and Ruth have strong feelings about giving to charities and missions they have worked with during the last 20 years. However, they must be careful not to enrich charities and deprive their children. They certainly don't want to embitter their children to the point where they may be driven away from a relationship with God. Communicating with your family about the motivation behind your decisions serves to open up discussion and avoid the opportunity for bitterness. .

The moderator may be used to direct the discussion. The participants are the parents, the children (with perhaps their spouses) and perhaps older grand children. How early should you have the family conference depends on the maturity of your children and the items you want to discuss with them. Those who have had family conferences to discuss the wealth transfer rarely regret it.

You might think your assets are too small to merit talking with the family. On the other hand you may feel that your situation is too large and complicated. My feeling is you can never err when you are talking about these issues. The smallest of the items... a picture of the old home place, a small table, a set of China... can cause sparks to fly amongst the heirs after death; therefore, they should be talked about when we are all alive.

An example of a benefit of the family meeting might involve inherited wealth. I have seen this happen, many times the persons who inherits property feels obligated. Perhaps it is a stock you inherit from Granddad. Granddad loved the stock and felt it was the best stock to own. I could never sell it because granddad wouldn't want me to. The heir becomes paralyzed when managing these inherited assets. A family meeting can help clear the air on mom and dad's feeling so that more mature, intelligent decisions may be made concerning these assets.

Chapter 11
Final Destination...

Congratulations, you have completed the Roadmap to Getting Your Financial House In Order. I dare say you are among a small percent of the population in America who have addressed all of the items mentioned in our journey. I think you'll agree it is not enough for Ted and Ruth to read this material. The important thing is to have put this information into action. Ted, knowing he needed to name Ruth as his primary beneficiary on his $250,000 Sunoco life insurance policy isn't enough. If he did not change the beneficiary the wrong person would receive the $250,000. Every step along the roadmap requires action. Don't just be a listener only, be a doer.

Another suggestion is an active commitment to monitor your plan. Our roadmap has taken us to a number of different issues. We live in a dynamic world which is constantly changing. Things change and you need to be willing to adopt and change where appropriate. There is no right or wrong timing on monitoring your plan.

God gives you common sense so put it to use as you think about every aspect of your roadmap. Some things, like your investment portfolio, needs to be monitored on a quarterly or semi-annual basis. Other items such, as your will and trust may only need to be addressed every three to five years (assuming there is no major change in your situation). The important thing is not to put your plan on the shelf and leave it there.

In addition, I suggest you surround yourself with competent advisors. We've discussed the advisors throughout the roadmap journey. Most people will need a competent accountant, a competent estate planning attorney, a competent financial planner and finally a competent property and casualty insurance person. You notice I repeated the word competent before each profession. After five decades in this business, I have seen too many incompetent people giving advice. Take the time to make sure the people you are working with... your team members... are competent. Is it enough just to like or to trust them? No!! People liked and trusted Bernie Madoff. There are a number of likable, untrustworthy people roaming around. Do your homework and make sure they deserve your trust. At the least they should have a professional designation with no complaints within their professional organization and five years of experience in their specialty.

In the last section of the book, I have provided reference material and forms you may use in developing your own roadmap.. These are available for you to take action. Feel free to make copies of any of these forms for yourself or others who may benefit from them. Should you have questions or need additional information, please check our website at F-P-R.com or email me at james.nichols@natplan.com. Should you have questions I will be pleased to visit with you by phone (919 494-2929).

God bless you and have a wonderful life.

Appendix
Investment History 1802 thru 2002

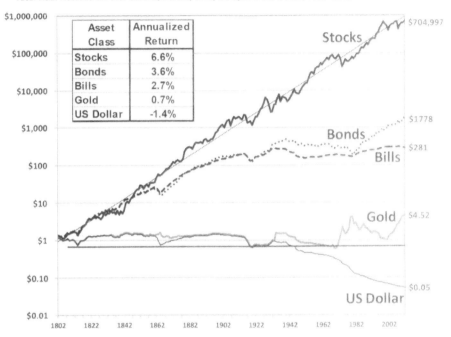

Total Real Returns on U.S. Stocks, Bonds, Bills, Gold, and the Dollar, 1802–2012

Asset Class	Annualized Return
Stocks	6.6%
Bonds	3.6%
Bills	2.7%
Gold	0.7%
US Dollar	-1.4%

Source: (Part II Verdict of History) **Stocks for the Long Run**, by Jeremy J. Siegel

Personal Financial Data Form – Introduction

The following data is strictly confidential. The information will be analyzed by one of our representatives, and you may receive a personalized analysis that will help answer the important questions listed on the cover. The analysis might also provide the basis for making recommendations for specific investments and other financial tools that you should consider to help meet your family's needs and pursue your goals.

Instructions: For purposes of identification, list the individual with the larger annual income as Client A. The individual with the lesser income, or a nonworking spouse, should be listed as Client B. When entering figures, use only the dollar amounts. Do not include cents. If you are unable to complete some sections or have questions, write "please call" in the margin and your advisor will consult with you prior to developing your financial analysis.

Section 1. Family Data   Today's Date _____

PERSONAL DATA:	FIRST NAME	M.I.	LAST NAME		Age	Sex	Year of Birth
Client A							
Client B							

Do you use tobacco products?   Client A ❏ Yes ❏ No   Client B ❏ Yes ❏ No

Home Address:

Street		
City	State	Zip
Phone # 1 ( )	Client A Business ( )	Fax Number ( )
Phone # 2 ( )	Client B Business ( )	Fax Number ( )
Email Address		

Children: * First Name	M.I.	Age	Sex	Year of Birth	College Funding**	Age to Start	Total Yrs. in School	Current Cost/Year	Amount Already Saved
					❏ Yes ❏ No				
					❏ Yes ❏ No				
					❏ Yes ❏ No				
					❏ Yes ❏ No				
					❏ Yes ❏ No				
Dependent					❏ Yes ❏ No				
Dependent					❏ Yes ❏ No				

* If you plan to have children, or additional children, please write "Planned" in the dependent space and indicate the approximate future birth date(s).

** If you anticipate paying for your children's college education, choose Yes.
If you do not specify a cost for education in today's dollars, we will use the average cost of a public four-year college.

Section 2. Professional Information

Client A:	Client B:
Occupation	Occupation
Employer Years	Employer Years
Check here if ❏ Retired ❏ Self-Employed	Check here if ❏ Retired ❏ Self-Employed

Name/Firm	Telephone
Accountant	( )
Attorney	( )
Financial Advisor	( )

Section 3. Investment Objectives

The following information is necessary in order to develop an analysis that, when implemented, should reflect your expectations for the future, meet your needs, and be consistent with your temperament, goals, and objectives. Many factors must be considered before deciding what type of investments should be made and how much of each to purchase. Most important, however, are your own goals and risk tolerance levels.

DESIRED INVESTMENT FEATURES
Put a check mark (✓) in the box in each row that best describes your attitude toward investing.

Investment Objective/ Characteristic	How important/acceptable is this objective/characteristic to you?				
	Extremely	Highly	Moderately	Slightly	Not
High Total Return					
Long-Term Deferred Gains					
Tax Benefits					
Current Income					
Stability of Principal					
Absence of Short-Term Losses					
Liquidity					

AVERAGE ANNUAL INFLATION RATE: We will base our calculations on a _____ % inflation rate, unless you specify a higher or lower rate in the space that follows: _____ %.

MONTHLY GROSS INCOME DESIRED AT RETIREMENT, PRETAX, IN TODAY'S DOLLARS:
Please list the income desired for retirement when both Client A and Client B are retired. $_____

RETIREMENT CONSIDERATIONS	Client A	Client B
Planned retirement age		
Already retired?	❏ Yes ❏ No	❏ Yes ❏ No
Do you want us to figure Social Security as part of your retirement benefits?	❏ Yes ❏ No ❏ Not Eligible ❏ Reduced Rate ____%	❏ Yes ❏ No ❏ Not Eligible ❏ Reduced Rate ____%
Are you a participant in the Federal Employee's Retirement Plan?	❏ Yes ❏ No	❏ Yes ❏ No
Are you a participant in the Railroad Retirement Plan?	❏ Yes ❏ No	❏ Yes ❏ No
A life expectancy of 85 years is assumed for planning purposes. List an alternative age, if desired:		

Section 4. Cash Reserves Detail

Investment Type: CK = Checking Account; MI = Money Market Interest Account; MM = Money Market Fund; SA = Savings Account; TB = U.S. Treasury Bills

Name of Institution	Owner (A, B, or Both)	Investment Type	$ Current Balance	Interest Rate

Amount of Personal Property* You Own: $_____

*Personal property includes your home furnishings, autos, boats, antiques, heirlooms, jewelry, silver place settings, stamp collections, etc., that you do not want to sell to fund your retirement needs. Investment items such as gold and silver bullion or coins, investment-quality diamonds, investment real estate, and other collectibles should be included with your investment assets in Section 5. Personal property should be listed at fair market value. All loans against personal property should be listed in the Liabilities section.

Section 5. Investment Detail List all variable annuity and variable life insurance information in Section 7. 2

Account Type: If this investment is not held in a tax-deferred account such as those listed below, then leave this column blank.

FA = Fixed Annuity
I = IRA
K = Self-Employed Plan
P = Profit Sharing or 401(k)
S = SEP-IRA

FG = 457 Plan
T = 403(b)
U = Universal Life Insurance Policy Cash Value
W = Whole Life Insurance Policy Cash Value

Investment Type:
CB = Corporate Bond
CD = Certificate of Deposit
F = Fixed Account
GS = U.S. Treasury Notes & Bonds
MB = Municipal Bond
MF = Mutual Fund

MM = Money Market Fund
OG = Oil & Gas Limited Partnership
SA = Savings Account
RE = Real Estate Limited Partnership
S = Stock
T = Tangible Assets*
TB = U.S. Treasury Bills
TS = Other Tax Shelters

Name	Account Type	Investment Type	Owner (A, B, or Both)	Current Value	Annual Return	Margin Debt	# of Shares	Maturity Date	Purchase Price	Date of Purchase

Continue in Section 15, Additional Information, if necessary.

*Tangible assets are investment items not considered personal property, such as gold and silver bullion or coins, investment-quality diamonds, and other collectibles that will eventually be sold and used to fund your retirement needs.

Section 6. Present Life Insurance Type: T = Term; U = Universal Life; V = Variable Life; W = Whole Life 3

Insurance Company Name	Type	Insured A, B, or Child's Name	Beneficiary A, B, Other	$ Face Amount	$ Cash Value	$ Loans Against	Loan % Rate	$ Annual Premium
	Group Term	Client A						(if any)
	Group Term	Client B						(if any)

When you return this data form, enclose your Life, Disability, and Long-Term Care Insurance Policies, and any other policies you would like your advisor to review. It will be very difficult for your advisor to accurately analyze your insurance program without these policies.

Section 7. Variable Annuity and Variable Life Insurance Detail 3

Account Types: VA = Variable Annuity; VL = Variable Life Insurance Cash Value
Subaccount Types: B = Bonds; F = Fixed Account; M = Money Market; R = Real Estate; S = Stocks

Insurance Company Name	Owner (A, B, or Both)	Beneficiary (A, B, or Other)	Account Type	Subaccount Type	Name of Subaccount	Contract or Cash Value Amount	Annual Return

Copyright © 2002, 2015 SMMS, Inc.

Section 8. Employer Monthly Benefit Pension Detail (Your employer can help you determine this information.)

Are you eligible to participate in an employer-sponsored retirement plan?　Client A: ❏ Yes　❏ No　Client B: ❏ Yes　❏ No　**3**

Owner (A or B)	Monthly Benefits Expected	Year to Start Benefits	Year to Finish Benefits	Rate of Increase (if any)	Death Benefit to Survivor (monthly)

Section 9. Money Owed You　**3**

Original Amount	Owner (A, B, or Both)	Original Date	Original Term	Interest	Current Balance	Monthly Payment

Section 10. Real Estate Portfolio Detail　**3**

Real Estate Type:
PR = Primary Residence　I = Investment Property
SR = Second Residence　O = Other
R = Recreation Property

Mortgage Number:
F = First
S = Second

Credit Insurance:
D = Disability Insurance　B = Both Disability and
L = Life Insurance　　　　Life Insurance
N = None

Type	Owner (A, B, or Both)	Market Value	Equity	Annual Property Tax	Mortgage Number	Original Mortgage Amount	Date of Mortgage	Term (Years)	Mortgage Balance	Monthly Payment	Interest Rate	Credit Insurance A	Credit Insurance B

Section 11. Liabilities　Do not include real estate loans in this section. All real estate loans should be entered in Section 10.

Credit Insurance: D = Disability; L = Life; B = Both; N = None　**4**

Item or Company Name	Original Date	Original Amount	Original Term	Balance	Interest Rate	Minimum Payment	Current Payment	Credit Insurance Client A	Credit Insurance Client B
Auto Loan 1									
Auto Loan 2									
Auto Loan 3									
Recreational Vehicle									
Credit Card									
Credit Card									
Credit Card									
Line of Credit									
Student Loan									
Other									
Other									
Other									

Section 12. Income Data Detail

PRESENT INCOME (Pretax Annual)	Client A	Client B		Client A	Client B
1. Salary/Wages and Bonus			8. Rental, Royalty, or Partnership Income		
2. Annual Salary Increase %			9. Income from Trusts		
3. Net Income from Self-Employment			10. Social Security Benefits		
4. Taxable Interest Income			11. IRA/Self-Empl. Plan Distrib./Withdrawals		
5. Tax-Exempt Interest Income			12. Pension or Annuity Income		
6. Dividends			13. Other Income		
7. Capital Gains			14. TOTAL PRESENT INCOME	$	$

Do you anticipate any major changes to your income in the next two years? ❏ Yes ❏ No

If yes, explain: _____

Section 13. Income Tax Data

FILING STATUS: (check one) ❏ Married/Joint ❏ Single ❏ Head of Household ❏ Married/Separate

1. Total Present Income from Section 12, Line 14 (Total for both clients)	$	6. Nontaxable Income (Social Security benefits, tax-exempt interest, etc.)	
2. IRA Deduction Client A: ____ Client B: ____	Total	7. Other Adjustments	
3. Self-Empl. Plan/SEP Deduction Client A: ____ Client B: ____	Total	8. Adjusted Gross Income (line 1 minus lines 2, 3, 4, 5, 6, 7)	
4. 401(k)/403(b) Plan Contribution Client A: ____ Client B: ____	Total	9. Itemized or Standard Deductions	
5. Cafeteria Plan Contribution Client A: ____ Client B: ____	Total	10. Exemptions (#)	

FAMILY NET TAXABLE INCOME (Line 8 minus 9 & 10) $ _____ Tax Credits $ _____ Year _____

TOTAL TAXES PAID LAST YEAR: Year _____ Federal $ _____ State $ _____ FICA $ _____

Section 14. Anticipated Future Income

DESCRIPTION: B = Bonus; D = Deferred Compensation; E = Early Retirement/Severance Pay; I = Inheritance; L = Retirement Lump-Sum Distribution; R = Royalty; S = Sale of Business; O = Other

FREQUENCY: O = One Time; R = Recurring **PERIOD:** M = Monthly; Y = Yearly

Description	Owner (A, B, or Both)	Amount	Frequency	Period	Starting Year	Ending Year

Section 15. Additional Information

Continue on a separate sheet of paper, if necessary

Section 16. Monthly Cash Flow

A. SAVINGS & INVESTMENTS	$ Monthly	C. INSURANCE (continued)	$ Monthly
1. Savings Accounts, Money Market Funds		18. Homeowners/Renters Insurance	
2. Mutual Funds		19. Auto Insurance	
3. Stocks, Bonds, etc.		20. Other	
4. IRA/Self-Employed Plan/403(b)		21. TOTAL INSURANCE	
5. 401(k)/Profit-Sharing Plan Contribution		**D. STANDARD OF LIVING**	
6. Annuities		22. Housing (mortgage payments or rent)	
7. Other		23. Automobile/Transportation (gas, maintenance, and payments)	
8. TOTAL SAVINGS & INVESTMENTS		24. Debt Repayment (credit cards, other loans, etc.)	
Employer Ret. Plan Contribution Client A: _____ Client B: _____ Total		25. Food (groceries and dining out)	
B. TAXES		26. Medical/Dental (uninsured or not paid by insurance)	
9. Federal Income Taxes		27. Entertainment/Recreation/Vacation	
10. State Income Taxes		28. Education	
11. FICA – Social Security		29. Charity, Gifts	
12. Property Taxes		30. Clothing	
13. Other		31. Home Maintenance/Furnishings	
14. TOTAL TAXES		32. Utilities & Misc. Costs (phone, newspapers, etc.)	
C. INSURANCE		33. Unreimbursed Employee Business Expenses	
15. Life Insurance		34. Other	
16. Disability Insurance		35. TOTAL STANDARD OF LIVING	
17. Health/Dental Insurance		36. TOTAL MONTHLY BUDGET	

Section 17. Survivors' Needs

In today's economy, the death of either spouse can cause considerable financial hardship. We will automatically compute your insurance needs based on your present standard of living. If there are any special circumstances you would like considered, such as changes in your income or retirement age, please list them here.

Section 18. Other Insurance

Existing Coverage	Insurance Company Name	Monthly Benefits	% Increase, If Any	Waiting Period	Max. Benefit Period	Annual Premium
Disability Insurance Through Employer, Client A						
Disability Insurance Through Employer, Client B						
Personal Disability Insurance, Client A						
Personal Disability Insurance, Client B						
Long-Term Care Insurance, Client A						
Long-Term Care Insurance, Client B						

Section 19. Estate Planning

	Client A	Client B
Estate Planning strategies you use: (check all that apply)		
Credit Shelter Trust	❑	❑
Simple Will	❑	❑
Durable Power of Attorney	❑	❑
Buy-Sell Agreement	❑	❑
QTIP Trust	❑	❑
Annual Gifting (nontaxable)	❑	❑
Charitable Trust	❑	❑
Irrevocable Life Insurance Trust	❑	❑
Revocable Living Trust	❑	❑
Family Partnership	❑	❑
Taxable Lifetime Gifts	❑	❑
Other	❑	❑
If you checked "Other," please explain:		
If you have a will, when did you last review it?		
If you have a trust, describe:		
Have you made taxable lifetime gifts? If so, how much?		

Section 20. Other Goals and Needs

1. Amount, if any (in today's dollars), for your estate at your natural life expectancy: $ _____

2. Are any of your investment assets earmarked for any purposes other than retirement funding?
   If yes, please list. (Continue on Section 15, Additional Information, if necessary.)

3. Do you have any assets that you do not wish liquidated to fund retirement needs?
   If yes, please list. (Continue on Section 15, Additional Information, if necessary.)

4. How much can you afford to save each month in addition to what you are saving now? $ _____

5. The goal of financial analysis and investing is not simply to help you live comfortably in retirement. In many cases, a financial advisor can design a program for you that takes into account special considerations of needs other than retirement income. For each goal you wish to pursue, please specify whether it is a short-term goal (less than three years), medium-term goal (three to seven years), or long-term goal (more than seven years). Along with any goals you may have, please specify the amount in today's dollars you believe will be necessary to obtain this goal.

   If your specific goal is not listed, please include it on the blank lines at the end of the list.

	Short Term	Medium Term	Long Term		Short Term	Medium Term	Long Term
Purchase of home	___	___	___	Other	___	___	___
Purchase of vehicle	___	___	___				
Vacation/trip	___	___	___	Other	___	___	___
Purchase of boat/plane	___	___	___				
Purchase of second home/ recreational property	___	___	___	Other	___	___	___
Purchase of recreational vehicle	___	___	___				
Home maintenance/remodeling not covered in monthly budget	___	___	___	Other	___	___	___
Home furnishings purchase	___	___	___	Other	___	___	___
Medical expenses not covered by insurance	___	___	___				
Start own business	___	___	___				
Eliminate consumer debt	___	___	___				
Educational expenses	___	___	___				

Sample letter to confirm current beneficiaries

May be used for insurance companies or employer benefit departments

Insurance company name/employer name

Address

Re: Policy Number   Name of Insured/employee _____

                                    Name of owner _____

To Whom it may concern:

As owner of the policy I want to confirm the current primary and contingent beneficiary of the above policy (ies). Please send this information to your record of address.

Sincerely yours,

(the owner of the policy (or the employee) will need to sign the letter

Sample letter to request an Inforce illustration on your life insurance policy (ies)

Typically this is requested for cash value life insurance policies

Insurance company name

Address

Re: Policy Number   Name of Insured _____

                                Name of owner _____

To Whom it may concern:

As owner of the policy I want to request an Inforce Illustration on the above number policy (ies). Assume the current premium that I have been paying is continued. Also assume that the current interest/and or dividends continue to be credited to the policy. Run the illustration assuming I live to age 100. Please send this information to your record of address for me. Should you need additional information please contact me at this number _____.

Sincerely yours,

(the owner of the policy will need to sign the letter)

Sincerely yours,

(the owner of the policy (or the employee) will need to sign the letter)

INDEX

○ **Diversification:**

Neither diversification nor rebalancing nor any specific investment vehicle can ensure a profit or protect against a loss. Indices are unmanaged measures of market conditions. It is not possible to invest directly into an index. Past performance is not a guarantee of future results.

○ **Financial Strategy**

Prior to implementing any financial strategy individuals should consider their investment objective, time horizon, and tolerance for risk. Investors should also consider the fees and charges associated with implementation of any investment plan. No investment strategy can guarantee a profit or assure favorable results.

○ **Hypothetical illustrations**

Many factors determine the actual return on your investment and your actual investment return may vary greatly from the results offered by the hypothetical illustrations in this book. Please bear in mind that any calculation provided is meant only to provide an approximation and is not indicative of any particular investment, actual results will vary. Past performance is not a guarantee of future results.

○ **Methodology for: "Sustainable Withdrawal Rates Can Extend the Life of a Portfolio"**

These highlight varying levels of stocks, bonds, and short-term investments, the purpose of the hypothetical illustrations is to show how portfolios may be created with different risk and return characteristics to help meet a participant's goals. You should choose your own investments based on your particular objectives and situation. Remember, you may change how your account is invested. Be sure to review your decisions periodically to make sure they are still consistent with your goals. You should also consider all of your investments when making your investment choices.

○ **Municipal Bonds:**

In general the bond market is volatile, and municipal bonds carry interest rate, inflation, credit and default risks. Interest income generated by municipal bonds is generally expected to be free from federal income taxes and, if the bonds are held by an investor resident in the state of issuance, state and local income taxes. Such interest income may be subject to federal and/or state alternative minimum taxes. Investing in municipal bonds for the purpose of generating tax-exempt income may not be appropriate for investors in all tax brackets. Short and long term capital gains, and gains characterized as market discount recognized when bonds are sold or mature are generally taxable at both the state and federal level. Short and long term losses recognized when bonds are sold or mature may generally offset capital gains and/or ordinary income at both the state and federal level.

○ **Mutual Fund:**

Mutual funds are sold by prospectus. Investors should read the prospectus carefully and consider the investment objectives, risks, charges, and expenses of each fund carefully before investing. The prospectus contains this and other information about the investment company. Please contact your representative or the investment company to obtain the prospectuses.

o   Nonqualified withdrawals:

These do not enjoy tax-favored treatment. The earnings part of a nonqualified withdrawal will be subject to federal income tax, and the tax will typically be assessed at the account owner's rate, not at the beneficiary's rate. Plus, the earnings part of a nonqualified withdrawal will be subject to a 10 percent federal penalty, and possibly a state penalty too.

o   529 Tax- Free Provisions

An investor should carefully consider the investment objectives, risks, charges and expenses associated with 529 plans before investing. More information is available in the issuer's official statement which can be obtained from your financial professional. The official statement should be read carefully before investing.

Most states offer their own 529 programs, which may provide advantages and benefits exclusively for their residents and taxpayers. The investments inside a 529 plan may fluctuate with changes in market conditions and when redeemed shares may be worth more or less than their original value.